LEARNING TO LOVE:

JOURNEYS THROUGH LIFE WITH THE ROSARY

LEARNING TO LOVE

Journeys through Life with the Rosary

NIGEL WOOLLEN

VERITAS

Published 2018 by
Veritas Publications
7–8 Lower Abbey Street
Dublin 1
Ireland
publications@veritas.ie
www.veritas.ie

ISBN 978 1 84730 836 8

10 9 8 7 6 5 4 3 2 1

All Scripture quotations taken from the CTS *New Catholic Bible*, Catholic
Truth Society, Publishers to the Holy See, 2007.

Designed by Pádraig McCormack, Veritas Publications
Printed in Ireland by SPRINT-print Ltd, Dublin

Veritas books are printed on paper made from the wood pulp of managed forests.
For every tree felled, at least one tree is planted, thereby renewing natural resources.

Dedication

To the memory of Pat Fallon
(Roscommon & Galway, 1961–2018),
a faith-filled witness to God's kindness
and a friend to many

Contents

Acknowledgements

With thanks to Stuart for putting up with me in India,
Lindsay and Jude for always being there,
Kate and David for the garden room,
Léonie Scott-Boras (proof-reader *extraordinaire*)
and the Veritas team.

Gratitude for all who pray for priests,
and all who pray the Rosary.

Introduction:
You Shall Love the Lord, Your God

Party for Barty

'What do you want me to do for you?' Think about this question. If you were asked this, you'd certainly consider who was speaking and what talents or abilities they might have which could be useful to you. Far from the bland statement of 'If there's *anything* I can do ...' which sometimes masks a reluctance to get involved, the query 'What do you want me to do for you?' is serious: it requires a response. If the person asking is interested in your well-being, and if they have a certain measure of power or influence, wealth or connections, then it's worth formulating an honest reply.

Of course, this question is found in the Gospels (Mark 10:51 and Luke 18:41) and it's Jesus who poses it. Now if we believe that God speaks to each of us personally (and to all of us together as a community) through his Word in Scripture, then we can be sure that Jesus puts this question to us today. Is Jesus interested in our good? Definitely. Does he have power and wealth, and friends in high places? For sure. He is Lord of lords, the eternal Son of the Almighty Father, for whom all things are possible – and he works everything to the good of those who love him (cf. Romans 8:28). So we'd better think carefully about how we might respond to this simple query.

In the Gospel context, Jesus puts this question to a blind beggar, Bartimaeus – we'll call him Barty – who pleads with him as he enters Jericho. This disruptive beggar had disturbed some of the crowd by shouting at Jesus to have pity on him; they told him to be quiet. But 'Jesus stopped' (Mark 10:49): Jesus stops what he's doing when we call upon him with all our hearts! He asks them to call Barty to him, and Barty jumps up and runs to Jesus – not an easy thing to do when you're blind. So Jesus asks him, 'What do you want me to do for you?' Now we might think that Barty's problem is quite obvious, but Jesus wants to hear his answer. God knows all our needs, he's quite aware of every problem and fear we have, yet he loves to hear us formulate our desires. '"Master, let me see again." Jesus said to him, "Go, your faith has saved you." And immediately his sight returned and he followed him along the road' (Mark 10:51-52).

Just think: a blind man sees for the first time (or at least, the first time in years), and the first object of his gaze is the face of Jesus. As a reward for his faith in this 'Jesus' he had heard about – and for his patient acceptance of his state in life – he now sees, and he sees his Master, the one who comes to restore and heal; 'I have come so that they may have life and have it to the full' (John 10:10). Now Barty is made whole, he won't need to sit begging anymore, so what does he do? *He follows Jesus along the road!* He has encountered the one who is Life itself, who invites us to the banquet of heaven, the great celebration of joy and laughter which will never end – a party for Barty, we could say. So Barty is now on a journey, which will lead to eternal life, because he follows Jesus, who is the way to the Kingdom.

We, too, could do worse than answer this question with, 'I want to see' – to see what really matters, to see beyond the often dark or sad appearances of this broken world or of our own battered lives. To see the greatness of our vocation to love, and ultimately, to see the glory of God (cf. John 11:40). The life of heaven is often called the *beatific vision*: 'what we are to be in the future has not yet been revealed … we shall be like him, because we shall see him as he really is' (1 John 3:2). If we give him our blindness, our inability to see heaven present in our midst, he can lift the veil to give us a glimpse of something beautiful which lies beyond – then, if we follow him along the road, we're already on the right path to living life to the full.

Jesus' question impels us to take a look at our own lives. What do I really want? How can I be happy? Where does my heart find rest? 'If you find your delight in the Lord, he will grant your heart's desire' (Psalms 36:4). That's all well and good, but what if I don't even know what my heart's desire is? Well maybe I do, deep down: it's to love and be loved. Loving is difficult, even impossible for us deeply wounded human beings. Yet, 'nothing is impossible to God' (Luke 1:37). How can I learn how to love? God is love, we've heard that somewhere (cf. 1 John 4:8). The problem is that we yearn to love, yet we fall short. We want to be loved, accepted and welcomed for what we are, but in an imperfect world, true love seems hard to find. Then what's the answer?

You shall love
The Word of God can shed light on all our deepest questions; however, we need to engage with it and let God

speak to us through it. 'Listen, Israel: The Lord our God is the one Lord. You shall love the Lord your God with all your heart, with all your soul, with all your strength. Let these words I urge on you today be written on your heart. You shall repeat them to your children and say them over to them whether at rest in your house or walking abroad, at your lying down or at your rising' (Deuteronomy 6:4-7).

We've heard of the Ten Commandments, also called the *Decalogue* or Ten Words, given by God to Moses on Mount Sinai (Exodus 20:1-17, see also the *Catechism of the Catholic Church*, or CCC, 2083). We might sometimes struggle to reel off the list, but deep down, all of God's commandments are contained in the very first one: 'You shall have no gods except me' (Exodus 20:3) – if we only kept that one, we would be on the right road to the kingdom! The tendency to allow ourselves to be enticed by other things, which then become our gods, is a sad reality in each of our lives and in world history. Relationships, material goods, earthly pleasures, the need to be in control and all kinds of distractions – all these aspects of our fragmented daily existence are not necessarily bad in themselves, but can make us forget the one supreme good, our God. He calls us into an extraordinary, loving relationship with him, which brings meaning and value to all our other friendships, and to every aspect of our lives.

The Decalogue is preceded by a statement which we can sometimes miss but which is crucial to our understanding of God's commandments, and of the whole Christian life: 'I am the Lord, your God, who brought you out of the land of Egypt, out of the house of slavery' (Exodus 20:2). If we begin by acknowledging the Lord our God, who has set us free from slavery to sin and leads us to the Promised land, then we see the commandments not just as prohibitions ('Don't do that!') but as *promises*: If you live like this, then you will be truly human; truly free!

What God is saying in the commandments – in all his commandments – is this: If you accept me as the God who frees you from slavery, if you welcome me as the centre of your life, then you will be empowered to live the commandments and discover a real freedom in keeping my precepts. Then you will become what I've wanted you to be from all eternity.

This means that if we put God first in our hearts, the 'shall not' of each of the ten commandments doesn't just express 'you're not allowed to' but 'you will not want to', 'you will be protected from the desire to' have other gods, to kill and steal, to desire what is another's, and so on. A whole new way of understanding God's ways opens up to us. Jesus echoes and completes the Decalogue in the Gospel when he says (just after teaching his disciples the Beatitudes and the *Our Father*): 'Set your hearts on his kingdom first, and on his righteousness, and all these other things will be given you as well' (Matthew 6:33). Righteousness can be understood here as God's faithfulness to his covenant promises to us in his Son, which invites us to strive to be faithful to him in return.

Our inner place

This brings us on to the *Shema* (which means to 'hear' or 'listen' in Hebrew), the passage of Deuteronomy quoted above, which is still recited each day by pious Jews. We can read it as a string of commands, as the things that we have to do in order to be pleasing to God, and while this is correct it's incomplete. Again, the opening verse is crucial: 'Hear, O Israel: The Lord our God is one Lord' – our God is speaking to us, and we are enabled to hear what he is saying. We are *capax Dei*: we have a capacity for God. Our greatest dignity as human beings is based on the reality that we are called to communion with God (cf. CCC 27). When we go into our inner place, we discover the one Lord who dwells in our hearts, and his command becomes promise: you *shall* love the Lord your God.

The drama of human existence is that we were created in order to welcome God's infinite love and to respond by loving him – and each other – with all our heart and soul, but we fall short every day. Our greatest handicap in life is that *we don't know how to love*! If only we could learn how to hear him speaking to us, so that his gentle voice would guide us in all our actions. Then we would discover his love filling our hearts and minds, thus empowering us to grow in that love. God is faithful; he keeps his promises and never takes back his gifts (cf. Romans 11:29). If we believe that he speaks to us – always through his Son Jesus, who came to show us how to listen to the Father and how to live to the full – then we must trust that he'll make our hearts grow to love as he loves.

The passage continues: 'These words which I command you this day shall be upon your heart; and you shall teach them diligently to your children'. Jesus promised to those who believed in him: 'If you make my word your home, you will indeed be my disciples, you will learn the truth, and the truth will make you free' (John 8:31-32). If we allow his word to enter our hearts, we will discover the truth – the truth that we are loved, that we were created for love and real happiness; the Truth, who is a person, the very Word of God for whom we were made – and we will be able to walk the path of true freedom. Then our lives will speak to others of God's love; our 'children' can be those we meet who are hungering for life, meaning and authentic love.

However, we need patience: life is a journey or a pilgrimage, with different stages we have to walk through in order to reach the promised land of true love and freedom. The *Shema* indicates these stages immediately afterward: You 'shall talk of them when you sit in your house, and when you walk by the way, and when you lie down, and when you rise'– here we have a plan for life, not just the various kinds of actions making up our day, but four stages in our lifelong journey of learning to love.

A Road Map: The Rosary

But we need a map! So why the Rosary? It enables us to meditate on the Gospel, the key events in salvation history, together with Mary who was given to us by Jesus as our Mother (cf. John 19:25-27). She welcomed the Word in her heart and helps us to do the same. Pope Francis reminded us in Fátima (in 2017), quoting Blessed Paul VI, 'If we want to be Christian, we must be Marian'. Francis then said, 'Each time we recite the Rosary, in this holy place or anywhere else, the Gospel enters anew into the life of individuals, families, peoples and the entire world'.

As we will see, the four stages of our journey correspond neatly with the four sets of Rosary mysteries:

* *When you sit in your house*: everything begins with an encounter, meeting the Lord who is love. The Lord comes to our home, our inner place, to tell us we're loved and to show us that there is a plan for our lives. The *Joyful Mysteries* show us how Mary's encounter with the Lord led to salvation for the whole human race, and how our lives are a part of this beautiful story of redemption.

* *When you walk by the way*: having encountered the love of God, we can't keep it to ourselves, we must share it. This is the mission of the Church, which sends out apostles of God's mercy to the world. The *Luminous Mysteries* (or *Mysteries of Light*) help us to reflect on Jesus' three-year public ministry, beginning with his Baptism and leading to the Eucharist, the great sign of our Master's love for each one of us. The sacraments, therefore, are an integral part of the apostolate.

* *When you lie down*: we tend to think of life's limitations, illnesses and all kinds of trials as obstacles to our effectiveness in sharing the Good News. The *Sorrowful Mysteries*, however, remind us that suffering can be the

greatest apostolate of all: by the passion and death of Jesus, redemption is won for all. When we think about what Jesus did for us by dying on the Cross, we are empowered to see our pains in a new light: nothing is wasted if it is united to his life. No struggle is pointless because he has given all our struggles new meaning by his passion, through which he redeems the world and opens the gates of heaven to us sinners.

* *When you rise*: for the Christian, death is not the end, as we believe that Jesus rose again as a pledge and guarantee of our own resurrection. The *Glorious Mysteries* inspire us to live, here and now in the hope of the happy ending for all believers. Christ died and rose for us, in order to give us new life, life in the Spirit. Our world needs hope, maybe more so today than ever before. By learning to welcome the Holy Spirit as Mary and the Apostles did, we can become witnesses to this hope which does not disappoint (cf. Romans 5:5). As we wait for the Lord to return, we strive to grow in the hope that he will transform creation into what he wanted it to be from the beginning. God is faithful; if we let him work, he will bring to completion the work he has begun in us and in the world. If others see believers living in joyful anticipation of paradise, they will be drawn to want this new life too.

Keep practising!

'I'm a practising Catholic,' a friend once said to me. 'I haven't got it right yet, but I'm still practising!' The same could be said for all those who want to love: we may not have 'got it right yet' but we have to keep practising, trying and learning.

In 2017, Pope Francis confirmed the heroic virtues of a remarkable Irish priest, Fr Patrick Peyton (1909–92), thus declaring him 'venerable'. Known as the Rosary Priest, Fr Peyton, born in Co. Mayo, conducted massive Rosary rallies throughout the world, yet never forgot his humble origins and the grace of God guiding him. Perhaps one day he'll be known as St Patrick of Co. Mayo; may his example inspire a new generation of families and young people to tap into the power of the Rosary, enabling them to experience more fully God's love for his children.

This book is written for those who already recite the Rosary, to help foster their meditation, and also for those who haven't yet discovered the depths of this powerful prayer, yet want to learn to love. It has been written so that all of us may grow in our desire for heaven and experience the joy of the Gospel. May our Mother Mary be at our side to help us on this journey, since she always leads us to the heart of the Gospel, the Heart of her divine Son.

I. When You Sit in Your House

Encountering the Lord – Joyful Mysteries
The Lord Comes to Our House: Called and Chosen

1. The Annunciation: Learning to Receive (Luke 1:26-38)

'In the sixth month the angel Gabriel was sent by God'. This is where our journey begins. The focal point of the meeting of the Most High God with the human race is found here, in an encounter between his messenger – the archangel Gabriel – and this young woman of Nazareth, whose name is Mary. Through the Gospel account, we are invited into Mary's home in this small town of Palestine, to witness a key event of salvation history, which culminates in the incarnation of the Son of God into our world; an event which also sheds light on our encounters, our journeys, and God's saving plans for each one of us.

Mary is sitting at home. In her house, surely a modest, simple dwelling, everything breathes loving silence. If our homes say something about who we are and how we live, then Mary's home certainly speaks of love, simplicity and welcome. We feel at home straight away. There's no need for words; we feel loved, drawn into silence, and accepted just as we are. In the Virgin of Nazareth, who from her very origins was already prepared for her unique mission, we find harmony – the harmony of one who lives with God, whose every breath is drawn out of love for her Creator. 'Your name is an oil poured out,' sighs the bride in the Song of Songs (1:3). As one who lives to honour the name of the one true God, Mary's love, as if poured out, spreads tangibly through her dwelling, inviting us therein, stirring up in our being a desire for authentic love, a yearning to possess something of the divine perfume which we sense filling our surroundings.

Mary is described as 'a virgin betrothed to a man named Joseph' – she already had plans, before the visit of the angel;

this is important. Like all the young Jewish women of her day, she would be expected to marry and bear children – a human and religious duty, for one day the long–awaited Messiah would be born of his people. Gabriel comes to propose a much greater plan – unthinkable and unexpected – yet he doesn't oppose her own: God's plan will unfold through Mary's marriage to Joseph, yet in an entirely new way. We might have had plans, even before we ever met God or were aware that he had designs for our lives. He comes not to cancel out our projects, but to make them into something even better, if only we would welcome him into our home, our inner space which he wants to fill with his loving presence; 'Oh that today you would listen to his voice! Harden not your hearts' (Psalms 94:7-8). When we listen to his voice with a heart open to his plans for us, we discover that 'his power, working in us, can do infinitely more than we can ask or imagine' (Ephesians 3:20).

Rejoice!

The very first word of the celestial messenger is the simple greeting of Mary's culture, *shalom* (or its Aramaic equivalent) implying peace, harmony and completeness – and is also an invitation to be joyful since the time of salvation is near. We could bear this ensemble of meanings in mind every time we pronounce the *Hail* of the Hail Mary. Whenever God enters into contact with us, he wants to bring joy, fulfilment and peace into our broken lives. We can glean something of Gabriel's joy here too: he contemplates the beauty of Mary, whose life and heart reflect the eternal perfectly. He rejoices in finding a human creature made in God's image who has never tarnished this image by any sin. She is 'most highly favoured,' full of grace – object of divine predilection from her earliest beginnings; and the angel will explain her mission, to bear the Son of the Most High, the one whose kingdom will have no end.

Mary is 'deeply disturbed,' not so much troubled as we would understand it when we're asked to do something that seems beyond our capacities. Rather, she is overwhelmed, somehow seizing the infinite gap between creator and creature, a chasm which seemingly she is being asked to cross. As the angel describes this Son she is asked to carry, and his destiny, she can be left in no doubt: this is the Anointed One announced by the prophets, the saviour of his people. How can this come about? Many Bible scholars see here an intimation of Mary's desire for total consecration; if her future marriage with Joseph was to involve bodily union, she wouldn't ask the question.

Gabriel explains: by the action of the Most High, in the power of the Holy Spirit, this child – the very Son of God – will be born of her. The mention of Elizabeth's unhoped for pregnancy confirms his message; we would think that news of her cousin's condition would have reached Mary in the previous six months. Gabriel wants to remind her that 'nothing is impossible to God.'

Saint Bernard meditates on this event in a melodramatic way, in which the whole of creation, the angels and the good souls of former times, yearning for their liberation, all await with bated breath the response of the Virgin of Nazareth. So Mary, the servant of the Lord, pronounces her *Fiat*: 'Let it be done to me according to your word'. Heaven and earth can be glad, for Mary's 'yes' changed the course of world history: God will become one of us. The Lord, who respects Mary's freedom, does not force his will but rejoices that she unites her free will with his eternal plan. A new era has dawned; a light shines in the darkness of this world, a light still hidden in Mary's womb, but which in the fullness of time will shine out to bring joy to all the earth.

'Yes' moments

We too are called to say 'yes' to love. Our 'yes moments,' in the small and great events of life, don't have the impact or consequences of Mary's; however, each yes to God's plan opens our hearts to love more, allying our life with his word. 'Your word is a lamp for my steps and a light for my path' (Psalms 118:105) – each time we say yes to his call, we see more clearly; the path lights up in front of us. Looking back, we can possibly identify situations of 'crisis' in our past – 'crisis' in the Ancient Greek sense means 'decision' or turning point – and it helps us see why a crisis (in the modern sense) can be an opportunity. I think of a young English priest I know, who obediently left his country for a new mission in Africa, and ended up welcoming the pope into his house. Then there was a French girl who rather unwillingly moved to Ireland, prompted by the Lord, not knowing that she would meet her husband there. When we say 'yes' to love, God's love can do great things.

An old priest who loved reciting the Rosary reached the point where he could barely speak; during each Hail Mary, all that could be heard from those close to him was: 'Ave … Jesus … Maria … Amen.' Those four words were surely enough; every *Hail Mary* renders present the angelic greeting, and reminds us that the Lord is with us. Every 'yes' offered with a generous heart affirms our courage – since Gabriel means *strength of God*, the God who repeats to us, 'Be not afraid.' Finally, in all our most impossible situations, for all the times when we don't understand what the Lord wants of us, he can simply state, *nothing is impossible to God*. May our Mother Mary, who kept all these things in her heart, help us to say 'yes,' and discover the joy of meeting God as our friend, who has wonderful plans for us and who will never let us down.

2. The Visitation: Bearing the Bearer of All Things (Luke 1:39-45)

'Mary set out at that time and went as quickly as she could to a town in the hill country of Judah.' She has encountered her Lord and is filled with joy, but she does not think of herself. She goes to meet her cousin Elizabeth – and Jesus goes with her. She 'bears the One who bears all things,' as the *Akathistos* hymn of the Eastern Churches proclaims; wherever Mary goes, her Lord travels too. As every unborn child is completely dependent on its mother, so the incarnate Word chooses to depend, to be carried – even though he is the one who carries the world in his heart. This smallness of God – who wills to depend, as if pleading for us to carry him and care for him – speaks to us more powerfully of his essence than all the grandeur of creation. Mary and her baby are one in love and joy; like every mother, she yearns to see his face and hold him in her arms, to feed him and watch him grow and mature. 'Of you my heart has spoken: "Seek his face"' (Psalms 26:8). But even now, before he is born, this Child is leading Mary to visit her cousin – his first apostolic mission on this earth, as St John Paul II remarked. Of course, she is going to help out her older relative during the latter's pregnancy, but there's something more in God's plan: we see from the few short verses of Luke's Gospel that an even greater mission is taking place.

Hello!

'As soon as Elizabeth heard Mary's greeting, the child leapt in her womb and Elizabeth was filled with the Holy Spirit.' This extraordinary event which (according to the Church Fathers) sanctifies St John the Baptist in his mother's womb and enables Elizabeth to be filled with the Spirit, begins with Mary's simple greeting. A mere 'hello' unleashes the Spirit and bestows grace; how can this be? It is because Mary is carrying Jesus, the Word made flesh, who comes to speak to us of the Father's love. The power of the word which created the universe (cf. Genesis 1) is now given to Mary; the Word cannot speak, yet he inspires his Mother to say a word, and as her whole being is a 'yes'

I. When You Sit in Your House

to love, that word has effect in the most profound way. Already in the Old Testament, prophets were anointed to speak on behalf of the Lord. 'Samuel grew up and the Lord was with him, and let no word of his fall to the ground' (1 Samuel 3:19) – when Samuel spoke, people listened, because God was speaking through him. If sometimes we don't feel listened to, we need to let God speak – which requires an inner silence – otherwise we will just be communicating our own thoughts and feelings, our own noise. Mary's silence allows the Word to be manifest, and her few words recorded in the Gospels attest to the power of God's life-giving message for those who are receptive. This helps us to understand why she is called *the Queen of Prophets*, which is not just another nice title but an affirmation of her singular prophetic calling, giving voice to the one who does not yet have a voice. We are also reminded that, in the world today, God has no voice but ours; through Baptism, we receive a prophetic mission, to speak God's word for society and for those we meet. This is a daunting responsibility; however, if Mary can produce such an outpouring of the Holy Spirit by simply saying *hello*, then we see what we need to do. If we learn to carry Jesus within us, in our hearts, then he will give us the right words at the right time: 'It is not you who will be speaking; the Spirit of your Father will be speaking in you' (Matthew 10:20). The visitation leads us, in a particular way, to the Eucharist: as Mary bore the divine Child in her womb for nine months with such love, she can help us to welcome him with love, every time we receive him in Holy Communion.

Elizabeth is now a partaker in the joy of the angel, shared by Mary, who welcomes the Saviour joyfully. Authentic joy is contagious, lighting up the lives of those in darkness. This encounter between friends, far from the madding crowd, lights up the world and inspires future generations to keep passing on the joy. Jesus wants to bless his older cousin who will be sanctified by a special grace even before his birth; the Lord can do this because the two women are open to life and joy. Elizabeth responds to the gift of the Spirit by proclaiming a blessing on Mary and on her baby; this blessing is repeated each day, countless times throughout the world. 'Blessed art thou among women, and blessed is the fruit of thy womb' – we could say, Mary is blessed *because* her Son is the Blessed, the Holy One of God. A blessing is, literally, a good word (*bene-diction*), yet the origin of its Hebrew equivalent suggests the 'knee' – it's as if the Father takes us upon his knee when he wants to bless us and tell us we're loved. 'Blessed be God the Father of our

Lord Jesus Christ, who has blessed us with all the spiritual blessings of heaven in Christ' (Ephesians 1:3): when we return to our Creator the blessing he has pronounced over our being, if only by reciting a Hail Mary, his blessings are multiplied and spread for us and for many around us. 'Why should I be honoured with a visit from the mother of my Lord?' Empowered by the Spirit, Elizabeth seems to recognise in faith the identity of this child her younger cousin is carrying, and expresses her wonderment at the gift of God. We can make her words our own. Whenever we pray the Rosary, Mary comes to visit us with her Son, to bring us joy and gladness. Mary is blessed because she believed in God's promise; when we welcome her presence, she can help us to believe in God, who has made promises for the lives of each one of us. We don't always see their fulfilment; but when we pray, we are given a glimpse of heaven, and a new impetus to become apostles of his love for those around us.

Baby Board

I have a file on my computer called 'Baby Board,' with due dates for the births of the babies of friends who are expecting, to remind me to pray for them. Every child conceived and destined to be born into the world – unique, immortal, sealed with the divine image – reminds us that God still has new plans for the human race and that he never tires of creating, giving new life. My friend Matthew was once 'pro-choice', but everything changed in an instant, when he saw the scan of his unborn daughter, and knew intuitively – even though he was then an atheist – that this was a new life, a unique gift to be treasured and protected. Matthew and his wife, along with many others like them, now work ardently for the protection of life in the womb in our society. This courageous apostolate finds its source in the presence of the Lord, who blesses all those who strive to speak the truth with love (cf. Ephesians 4:15). May our blessed Mother walk with us to enable us to be witnesses to life, thus illuminating a world so often in shadow. May her heart-to-heart with her Son be the guiding star of all our relationships, so that God's love, and not our own desires, may be the dynamic force in our lives.

3. The Nativity: Glory to God and Peace on Earth (Luke 2:1-20)

'At this time, Caesar Augustus issued a decree for a census of the whole world to be taken.' Luke's masterful arrangement of the material in his Gospel highlights the contrast between the great and powerful men of his time – the Emperor Augustus, Quirinius, the governor of Syria, and so on – with the arrival of the King of kings, the Lord whose reign will never end, yet who appears as a tiny child, unnoticed by the great ones of society. The timing seems inconvenient, to say the least, for the unfolding of God's plan: Augustus decides to undertake a census of his empire. This must have led to the displacement of huge numbers of people, all having to go to their town of origin to be registered – including Joseph, who has to set out with Mary, who is at the point of giving birth. For the Jews, taking a census, counting one's forces, implied a lack of trust in God's providence – as King David eventually realised (cf. 1 Chronicles 21). Mary and Joseph could have been tempted to murmur to the Lord, 'Don't you know we're expecting the Messiah? How could you let this happen right now?'

However, Mary and Joseph aren't the complaining kind; they leave quietly, for Bethlehem, the town of David – and this is where Jesus will be born, to fulfil an ancient prophecy: 'But you, Bethlehem, the least of the clans of Judah, out of you will be born for me the one who is to rule over Israel; his origin goes back to the distant past, to the days of old' (Micah 5:1). God has permitted a pagan ruler to call a census so that his Son would be born in Bethlehem! The name Bethlehem means 'house of bread,' and it is here that the Bread of Life will come into the world. So, we see how the Creator 'writes straight with crooked lines,' a constant theme of salvation history – which culminates in the passion of Jesus, whose death will bring new life for the whole world.

If Scripture is a mirror in which we can reread our own story, it's good to look back on our lives to see, often for the first time, how God worked through circumstances – in particular, all those events of our past which we saw only as negative, destructive, even absurd – to bring us to where we are today, and above all, to bring us to live in faith. *Blessed are you who believed*: Mary will constantly have to renew her act of faith, before the Herods, the Caesars, the Pharisees, and all those who seek to destroy her Son, he who came 'so that they may have life and have it to the full' (John 10:10). Every contradiction we undergo is an invitation to grow in faith. Thus, we become part of the great paradox of God's plan: he works out the salvation of the greatest number through paths that we can barely understand. All the details of our existence are important to him, nothing is trivial – therefore, what seems insignificant or even incomprehensible for us is all part of the divine working. God can post important messages through the (apparently) small events of our lives. 'His own designs shall stand for ever, the plans of his heart from age to age' (Psalms 32:11) – and we are in his heart.

My late father once recounted how he waited to be called up to the army at the tail end of World War II, having been posted to Burma. Just as he was due to set off, he was stricken with laryngitis – so his posting was delayed; he ended up being sent to Kenya! If the Burma posting had gone ahead, I might not have been born to write this. A friend to whom I told this tale remarked, 'I'll think about that next time I have a sore throat!'

News of great joy

So Joseph and Mary arrive in Bethlehem, where Mary gives birth to her child, and lays him in a manger 'because there was no room for them at the inn.' We know the story, re-enacted in countless Nativity plays throughout the ages. We could think about the coldness of those who have no time to welcome the Lord who is in their midst. Mary, however, wants us rather to grasp something of the joy of this holy night. For the first time in human history, mere mortals gaze upon the face of the hitherto unseen God, and the heavenly hosts of angels sing his glory. The shepherds, who represent the poorest of society, those living on the margins (and who also, surely, stand for priests), are the first to hear the good news, news of great joy. 'Glory to God in the highest heaven, and peace to those who enjoy his favour,' proclaim the angels – for now the Saviour is born for us. Mary and Joseph gaze with awe upon the Desired of the nations, the one 'through whom all things come and through whom we exist' (1 Corinthians 8:6). Just like any new parent who can barely take their eyes off their baby, Mary contemplates her son; she clasps him to her, welcoming this new relationship, offering him all the love of her heart – and in some way, she embraces each of her children to come, for she is destined to be Mother to each one of us. As Catherine Doherty – a Catholic social worker and founder of the Madonna House Apostolate – affirmed, *each person is an icon of Christ*: we are in his image, and he has become one of us in order to live and to die for each of us.

We know that King Herod will feel threatened by the announcement of this newborn king, and will take extreme measures, seeking to eliminate him (Matthew 2). The massacre of the innocents echoes the practice of the Egyptian Pharaoh in the Old Testament (cf. Exodus 1), who was motivated by his fear of the Hebrews whom he saw as a threat to his kingdom. In each case, slaughter of innocent ones precedes a new stage in God's plan: Moses is saved from the water (Exodus 2) to lead his people out of slavery through the waters of the Red Sea toward the promised land. Jesus, the new Moses, is exiled to Egypt in order to be safe from Herod's murderous intent, and will lead his people to the promised land of the kingdom, by means of the waters of Baptism. 'I called my son out of Egypt' (Hosea 11:1 and Matthew 2:15). Is the massive slaughter of the innocents of the last century a presage of a new stage in God's revelation? Only time will tell. It is not God who reacts to evil; rather, we might hazard a guess that the evil one, sensing the development of God's plans, works all the more furiously to influence earthly events – but love will always have the last word.

Song of silent love

What is the most universal song of all time? A strong candidate is the Christmas carol, 'Silent Night.' Originally a German song, it is now sung in as many as one hundred and forty languages around the world – I was reminded of this while listening to an Indian friend from Kerala singing its first verse in the Malayalam language last Christmas. The story of its composition two hundred years ago is almost a fairy tale in itself: according to one version, the church organ in Fr Joseph Mohr's Austrian village had been rendered out of action by some hungry mice. As a result the young priest sought out a local schoolmaster, Franz Gruber, to compose a melody (on his guitar) to lyrics he'd previously written. He did so, and the carol was performed for the first time that Christmas at Midnight Mass. The tale of the redundant organ may be later Hollywood fiction, yet it does ring true in some fashion: producing something beautiful out of apparent crisis is certainly in tune with God's way of working.

4. The Presentation: The New Temple (Luke 2:22-40)

'They took him up to Jerusalem to present him to the Lord.' It must have been busy in the Temple, with so many people coming to offer sacrifices, the temple priests slaughtering various animals – a noisy hub of activity. Not to mention the money-changers at their tables, possibly taking advantage of the poor folk coming from the country to make their offering, having saved whatever they could. Into this vast space of noise and commotion come Mary and Joseph, with little Jesus, just forty days old. They come in obedience to the Law of Moses, to consecrate their first-born son to the Lord. Yet this child is no ordinary child: he is the very dwelling-place of God on earth; whoever sees him sees the Father (cf. John 14:9). A revolution is occurring in the Israelites' worldview, since the Temple, their pride and joy, is now superseded by him for whom it was built. We hear in Luke's account the recurring phrase 'the law of the Lord' – which must be obeyed 'to fulfil all righteousness' (Matthew 3:15); now suddenly, the Holy Spirit bursts onto the scene, resting on the old man Simeon who awaits the consolation of Israel.

Simeon and the widow Anna may have been ignored by those running the temple business. Yet in the midst of this frenzy of activity, we find hearts at rest. The Holy Spirit who revealed to Simeon that he would set eyes on the Christ prompts him to enter the Temple. This old man with a youthful gaze is able to see beyond appearances, to recognise the Lord's anointed. His prophetic words bring wonder and consternation to Mary and Joseph: their child is destined for the fall and the rising of many, a sign of contradiction, 'so that the secret thoughts of many may be laid bare' (Luke 2:35).

By simply performing their religious duty, Mary and Joseph discover new horizons they could barely have imagined; Simeon's words, like every prophecy in the

Spirit, come not only to strengthen, but also to challenge them. They already hold within them the secret that this child is the Lord's envoy. Now they are asked to accept that the destiny of their son will have effects well beyond anything they can grasp. 'A sword will pierce your own soul,' Mary: even in the joy of welcoming new life, there is a shadow indicating what this child will have to undergo to bring salvation to his people – and not just for his people, 'but to gather into unity the scattered children of God' (John 11:52).

We see here a new stage of God's plan to live among his people: long ago, he had made his dwelling in the Temple of Jerusalem, in the Holy of Holies, into which only the High Priest could enter, and that only once a year on the Day of Atonement. The Temple, however, was provisional: it was to prepare God's children for the coming of his beloved Son, for 'in his body lives the fullness of divinity' (Colossians 2:9). So, the Presentation of the Divine Child in the Temple is a kind of homecoming. The Lord has indeed come to remain with his chosen people, in the fullest way possible. He comes, not to abolish (cf. Matthew 5:17) but to bring to perfection the Father's saving plans, 'not to condemn the world but so that through him the world might be saved' (John 3:17). By his loving purpose, we are called to something awesome, 'to share the divine nature' (2 Peter 1:4), something we could never have achieved by ourselves, yet offered to all as a free gift!

A future full of hope

I recently got a text message from a young mother whose daughter had just been born (by C-section) a month early; her mother said she hadn't held her yet. One can only imagine her pain and longing as she waits to hold her child in her arms. From the photo, I could see that her tiny treasure was in an incubator, covered in wires and linked up to monitors. I prayed to Mother Mary to help her. (Thankfully the child survived and is now doing fine.) When Mary holds the baby Jesus, and brings him into the Temple to hear prophetic words of joy and sorrow, she holds, in a certain way, each one of her children, as each child is in the image of her Son. 'The woman,' writes St Paul, in an oft-misunderstood passage, 'will be saved by childbearing' (1 Timothy 2:15): whereas circumcision was the ordinary means of marking out a Jewish male as part of the chosen race, women found their fulfilment, as members of Israel, through giving birth. So it was the duty of every Jewish girl to marry and procreate, to gain her salvation, and as we have seen, one of those children might be the Messiah. Saint Paul, however, takes a traditional precept to a new level: we can also translate the verse, 'The woman will be saved by the birth of the child,' this Child whose presence in our world brings redemption to all, women and men. And by the grace of Christ, every woman is called to motherhood of some kind; we can think of countless religious women (and many single women who live their faith ardently) whose lives consecrated to God in prayer and service spread grace and light – often in an unseen way – throughout society, thus bringing to birth many souls for the Kingdom. I once chatted to a young nun of an enclosed order. I'd just returned from a wedding, and discovered she knew the bride, so I showed her a photo of the happy couple on my phone. Sister sighed, remarking, 'To think I used to model wedding dresses.' This made me reflect on God's call, how he led a young woman from a promising career to what some would consider a 'waste' of a life – yet by following God, who calls certain souls into a deeper union with himself, she has become a light for the world, in a whole new way. 'I will betroth you to myself in faithfulness, and you will come to know the Lord' (Hosea 2:22).

During the liturgy of the Feast of the Presentation (2 February) each person holds a blessed candle, and we wait patiently as the candles are lit; the light coming from the Paschal candle spreads gradually from person to person until the whole church or chapel is filled with light. This is a powerful image of how God's love is handed on: as the light passes from one candle to another, so can we truly light up the world by our simple prayers and modest efforts for good. At the same time we receive the light God wants to shed on our own lives, helping us to see where he wants us to be, and find true fulfilment. As I heard a priest say during a funeral homily, 'If you combine prayer with acts of kindness, you will experience happiness and joy' – by spreading the light, we open up to God's loving designs for ourselves. 'I know the plans I have in mind for you – it is the Lord who speaks – plans for peace, not disaster, reserving a future full of hope for you' (Jeremiah 29:11). May the prayers of those who intercede for priests, vocations, and the light of God's love to spread be answered a hundredfold by our generous Saviour, who works all things for good if he finds faithful friends, willing to let their light shine.

5. The Finding in the Temple: In My Father's Company (Luke 2:41-52)

'Every year his parents used to go to Jerusalem for the feast of the Passover. When he was twelve years old, they went up for the feast as usual'. We wish the Gospel writers had included more details from the first thirty years of Jesus' life on earth, as he grew up, growing 'in wisdom and favour with God and men'. All we have is this passage, describing what happened when he was twelve, as Mary and Joseph went on pilgrimage to Jerusalem, as they did every year. Yet 'the boy Jesus stayed behind in Jerusalem without his parents knowing it' – of his own free will. It says much about the freedom enjoyed within the Holy Family, and the trust Mary and Joseph placed in their relations and acquaintances, that they only noticed he was missing after a day's journey on the road home. Of course, they looked for him everywhere; Luke's bare description, 'Three days later, they found him in the Temple' does not begin to describe the emotions suffered by these parents, who had lost not only their child but also their God.

We have seen that for Jesus, going to the Temple is going home, for he is the new Temple, the dwelling-place of the Most High, now made accessible for the chosen people. 'I am the Holy One in your midst,' the Lord had said through the prophet (Hosea 11:9). This was a paradox for Israel; how could the Holy One, utterly inaccessible to his people, be among them? Only now is the paradox resolved, yet by an even more incomprehensible action of God, becoming one of his people, in order to enter into a relationship with every person, so that we might know him as he truly is.

'My child, why have you done this to us?' This is the sole flicker of reproach recorded in the Gospels from Mary to her son. In a way, it is consoling for us to see that saints (even the immaculate one) experience moments of darkness and turmoil. So, did Mary worry? We can sometimes 'over-spiritualise' the events of the Gospel; for some Christians, all worry is sinful, resulting from lack of trust in God. Mary was sinless, therefore, was incapable of any feeling of anxiety. Her words – 'See how worried your father and I have been, looking for you' – would then be a tactful glossing over the fact that Joseph was desperately anxious while she glided dreamily through Jerusalem, confident that the boy Messiah would turn up. The reality is surely different: just as Jesus himself would experience 'sudden fear and great distress' in the garden before his passion (Mark 14:33), so Mary underwent the distress (the closest equivalent of the Greek word here, usually translated as *worry*) of losing her son, on behalf of all those who have had a similar experience, and in some way offering her solidarity to us for the times we have been unable to find our Lord. A mother I know who lost sight of her five-year-old son (for three minutes) in a Dublin shopping centre stated how those minutes felt like hours; the suffering of parents in similar situations is beyond the grasp of most of us. May St Josephine Bakhita intercede for them: she was abducted from her family, who never set eyes on her again, yet this woman of courage – now patron saint of Sudan, often cited by Benedict XVI – later recognised the work of Providence in her life story: 'If these things had not happened, I would not have been a Christian and a religious today'. We can take heart from the promise of Jesus to all who suffer: 'Your sorrow will turn to joy' (John 16:20).

'I must be busy with my Father's affairs' – this is hardly the response of a typical twelve-year-old. The doctors of the Law were astounded at his manifest wisdom (the passage implies that although Jesus is asking them questions, he is the one who gives the answers). Not that Jesus is the smart, know-it-all kid; he is Wisdom incarnate, living in perfect communion with the Father. Even if the human knowledge of Jesus during his time on earth is a much-disputed question, we can sense here that he is fully conscious of his mission, *to be in the Father's company*. They did not understand, but Mary 'stored up all these things in her heart' (Luke 2:51). Just as Joseph must let go of the son he adopted who now affirms his unique relationship with his heavenly Father, so must Mary grow in awareness of her own mission as Mother of the Redeemer. The bond between mother and son is unhampered by mechanisms of control (a mother's natural desire to retain a hold over her child who is growing up) or rebellion (the adolescent's desire to break free); Mary and Jesus together offer their 'yes' to the Father's will. There we find the template for all our relationships, whether those of family or friends. Jesus shows us the way: he invites us to be in the Father's company. There, we receive healing for broken relationships and the courage to never stop believing in love.

Long, long time ago

If we think about where we were twelve years ago, our circumstances were possibly very different, our worries and fears were quite unlike those we have now. For all parents concerned about their children, the problems seem to change as they grow up. For Mary, watching her child grow, every year brings new depths of joy to their relationship, but also an increased sorrow as she sees him set on the path which will inevitably lead to suffering and death. Twelve years seems a key time in the Gospels: we think of the 'two-in-one' story of the woman who'd suffered from a haemorrhage for twelve years; her clutching the

Lord's cloak in faith comes to interrupt his mission to raise Jairus' daughter (aged twelve) from the dead (Mark 5:21-43). So, the woman must have fallen ill around the time Jairus' daughter was born; they presumably never met, but their story is recounted anew in each generation, to remind us of the Father's omniscience and to illustrate the saving works of Jesus the Healer.

Called to the Temple

You may know the story of St John Vianney, who would spot the same farmer sitting praying each day in his small church in Ars, and asked him one day, 'What do you talk to God about?' The response of the peasant is usually translated, 'I look at him, he looks at me' – which is in itself a wonderful description of contemplative prayer. However, my French friends tell me that the verb used (for *look*) in the local Bressan dialect is the same one used to describe the way in which a farmer surveys a field he's about to purchase, to assess its value. We could thus render his reply: 'I size him up, he sizes me up!' This gives a new insight into our relationship with the invisible Friend. 'Didn't you realise that you were God's temple and that the Spirit of God was living among you?' (1 Corinthians 3:16). When we welcome Jesus, we are empowered to live, like him, in the Father's company, and we discover the deepest reality of what we are through Baptism: the temple of the living God.

Conclusion: Come down from your tree

Just by sitting in our house, we've come a long way. Helped by Mary's example and her joyful 'yes' to God's loving plan, we have encountered the Lord who visits us at home, bringing us into a healing relationship with himself. We discover that he loves us just as we are, and that he has great plans for our lives and our eternity; the smallness and gentleness of the Christ Child encourage us to go beyond our fears to meet him and get to know him as he really is. In addition, we learn something about our dignity as a beloved child of the Father, a brother or sister of Jesus and a temple of the Holy Spirit: whatever mistakes we've made, no one can take this dignity from us. To conclude the Joyful Mysteries, we can recall the story of Zacchaeus (cf. Luke 19:1-10), the little guy from Jericho with a big bank account (for he was a much despised tax collector) who climbed a tree to catch a glimpse of Jesus who was to pass by. When I visited the Holy Land, the guide proudly pointed out the very tree outside Jericho that Zacchaeus climbed (and who am I to doubt his word?) Jesus looked up and spoke to him, 'Zacchaeus, come down. Hurry, because I must stay at your house today'. *I must stay at your house*: this is the Lord's desire, to share our daily lives, transforming our sorrow into joy, for he can do all things. Each time we pray the Rosary, we receive the courage to come down out of our tree, to descend from pride and self-sufficiency to humble trust in his word. May Mary, the Mother of joys, be with us to remind us of the hope her Son imparts to his friends, and whisper to our hearts, 'Today, salvation has come to this house'.

II. When You Walk By the Way

The Apostolate – Mysteries of Light
*The Time of Mission: Sharing the
Love We Have Encountered*

1. The Baptism of the Lord: Learning to Walk (Mark 1:9-11)

'You are my Son, the Beloved; my favour rests on you'. When Jesus was baptised in the river Jordan by John, he saw the heavens torn open and the Holy Spirit descended upon him in the form of a dove – the symbol of peace, recalling how God renewed his covenant with the human race, represented by Noah, after the flood (cf. Genesis 8:11).

Of course, Jesus doesn't need to receive Baptism – a sign of repentance – since he is the eternal Son of the Father, the sinless one sent to take away the sins of the world. We can appreciate the Baptist's hesitation: 'It is I who need Baptism from you, and yet you come to me!' Jesus' reply is enigmatic: 'It is fitting in this way that we should do all that righteousness demands' (Matthew 3:14-15). God's righteousness (or saving justice) means his faithfulness to his covenant, his pledge of self-giving love, which invites our love in return. Jesus comes to turn all our ideas around. By receiving Baptism, he lifts up our wounded human nature, bestowing upon it a new dignity, an exalted state of being: through Baptism, we become God's beloved children. Precisely because Jesus was baptised, the Baptism we receive enables us to become by grace what he is by nature: a precious, unique child of the Father, a temple of the Holy Spirit, destined for glory.

'Your Catholic Church is fantastic!' a lady said to me recently. I don't hear that every day. She was preparing to be received into the Church at the following Easter Vigil. An incident in her story was that her car radio had broken: it was jammed on the Catholic station for several weeks – who said God doesn't have a sense of humour? Adult converts are a powerful reminder to all of us of the gift of God working in his Church. This woman – who declared that she doesn't want to be a 'submarine Catholic' (keeping one's faith out of sight, only surfacing when it's quite safe to do so) – will be a convincing witness to the love and mercy of God for others. We may sometimes be tempted to cling to the model of what I call the *Catholic factory*: working to produce identical little believers who all look and behave alike – but that's not God's way. In our times, the Lord is using extraordinary and creative means to bring his children to faith in him. Every story is different; each person is a mystery, and God brings each personality to flower in amazing ways, provided we let his grace in. As C.S. Lewis put it, 'How monotonously alike all the great tyrants and conquerors have been; how gloriously different are the saints'. And we're all called to be saints! Parents often tell me, with a sense of wonder, how different each of their children are, expressing a unique personality from their earliest years; how much more our heavenly Father sees the specific work of grace in each of his children. He longs for our uniqueness to be filled with his Spirit of love so that we can become the best versions of ourselves, fulfilling a role on this earth that he has in mind for us alone – and then shining one day in heaven with incomparable splendour.

Do you love me?

'You did not see him, yet you love him; and still without seeing him, you are already filled with a joy so glorious that it cannot be described, because you believe; and you are sure of the end to which your faith looks forward, that is, the salvation of your souls' (1 Peter 1:8-9).

How can we love someone without having seen them or met them? Saint Peter writes to newly-baptised believers to encourage them to persevere in difficult times. On the lakeshore after the Resurrection, it was Peter that Jesus looked at and asked, 'Do you love me' (John 21:15)? Peter must have been impressed by the love of these converts for the Jesus that they had never set eyes on as he had. He would have witnessed the gift of God's grace transforming those men and women, some of whom he had baptised himself – including St Clement, who later succeeded him as Bishop of Rome. Apparently, Peter noticed the joy of these disciples, 'so glorious that it cannot be described,' a joy which doesn't depend on material success or absence of trials (far from it) but whose reason is self-evident: 'because you believe.' Hadn't Peter himself heard Jesus say after his Resurrection, 'Happy are those who have not seen and yet believe' (John 20:29)? The goal of faith is 'the salvation of your souls' – not in a triumphalist way, feeling smugly content that we're saved, but in humble gratitude before the gift of God. Interestingly, the original Greek text doesn't have the word 'your' before 'souls' in verse nine, so we can also understand the end-point of the gift of faith as 'the salvation of souls:' this brings our faith journey to a whole new level, because it's not just 'me and my God.'

Every new believer who learns to love the Lord Jesus and walk in faith is already helping to bring souls to salvation since 'the life and death of each of us has its influence on others' (Romans 14:7). We all want to make the world a better place; the Kingdom is spreading throughout the world wherever there are people who pray and live out their faith in acts of kindness, enabling it to become what God wants it to be. This helps us to understand those disconcerting statements of certain saints, that Our Lady saved more souls by quietly sewing than all the martyrs put together, because she had more love. When we claim the joy that comes from walking with Jesus, we embrace the whole world; we discover the Christian sense of 'solidarity,' a fond term of St John Paul II, as a desire for communion with every person, who bears the image of the invisible God.

Crowd management

'Looking up, Jesus saw the crowds' (John 6:5) – we read this often in the Gospel. However, we know that Jesus didn't just see the crowd: in some way, he saw each wounded and broken disciple, hungering for life and love. He saw the choices each one had made, the efforts for good, the mistakes and wrong turns … and 'he took pity on them, because they were like sheep without a shepherd' (Mark 6:34). When we know that, despite all our faults, he looks at us and loves us, seeing our goodwill and our longing to do better, we can be joyful because his grace will make up for all that is lacking in us.

The largest crowd I experienced was during the World Youth Day gathering in Madrid in 2011. At the closing Mass, there were two million people, including fourteen thousand priests (and one pope). Being in a large crowd at a match or concert, you can experience a certain solidarity: you're with like-minded folk supporting the same team or enjoying the same music – but gathered together with the Lord, there's a communion which transcends human affinities; in his name, we are truly one. In heaven, the saints will be completely one in love and celebration, without any shadow of disharmony – yet each one will reflect God's love in a unique, unparalleled way: 'we, with our unveiled faces reflecting like mirrors the brightness of the Lord, all grow brighter and brighter as we are turned into the image that we reflect; this is the work of the Lord who is Spirit' (2 Corinthians 3:18).

2. The Wedding Feast of Cana: Trusting in Him (John 2:1-11)

'There was a wedding at Cana in Galilee.' Everyone loves a wedding: it is a solemn yet joyous activity, human and divine, during which a woman and a man commit themselves to each other for life, in love and fidelity, in response to God's plan; thus, they image the passionate love of God for his people. We've often heard the Gospel passage of the wedding feast of Cana read at wedding ceremonies. We should never tire of hearing our favourite Scripture passages, for Christ is present whenever the Word is proclaimed in the liturgy, and he always wishes to speak to us, sharing new dimensions of his loving plans, every time we hear his saving words. This event, recorded in St John's Gospel, has many layers of meaning – like all of Scripture, especially the four Gospels – but it's good to start with the reality which is occurring: there was a wedding! We know nothing about the happy couple: their names, what they did, or what their dreams were – just as in Psalm 44 (the 'Royal Wedding Song') which eulogises the king and his bride without divulging their identity, yet whose final flourish (verse eighteen) promises everlasting renown: 'May this song make your name forever remembered. May the peoples praise you from age to age.' All we can guess is that someone in the bridal couple's family circle knew Mary: 'the mother of Jesus was there.'

The only Mystery of Light in which Mary is present gives her a key role: she is named before Jesus and his disciples, who 'had also been invited.' In John's presentation of his Gospel, the first week of Jesus' ministry concludes with this marriage feast, linking it with the seven days of creation which culminate in the creation of man and woman and God's resting on the seventh day (Genesis 1:1-2:4). Marriage – the only one of the seven sacraments which existed before Christ (yet given a new status by him) – is a common biblical symbol of God's love for the human race calling us into a relationship with him. Jesus based several of his parables on the concept of the wedding banquet (e.g. Luke 14:7-11). Saint Paul meditates on the meaning of Christian marriage in a famous passage: 'this mystery has many implications, but I am saying it applies to Christ and the Church' (Ephesians 5:32). When the couple commit to a sacred bond which is free, faithful, fruitful and for their whole life long, they echo and reflect the love of God for all of us which itself is free, faithful, fruitful and for ever! Therefore, a married couple who strive to live out their vows can be wonderful witnesses to the faithful love of the Lord in the midst of society – but only with the grace of God! It is too easy to be cynical about marriage in our fragile world; yet Jesus and his Mother are there, to help men and women to be true to their commitments, working through the ups and downs of our lives to further his good plans for us.

Best for the end

At Cana, they ran out of wine – a disaster for a Jewish wedding, which could last several days. We could interpret this as symbolising love which is merely human, which will always be limited; divine action is required. Mary sees the need, and says quietly to her Son, 'They have no wine.' His response is mysterious, seemingly dismissive: 'Woman, why turn to me? My hour has not come yet.' Countless scholars have meditated on the meaning of these words; the general consensus seems to be that by addressing Mary as 'Woman,' Jesus (the new Adam) is recalling the first woman, Eve, as if to suggest that the new creation is dawning. Later, from the Cross (John 19:26), he will call her by the same term, entrusting her to his beloved disciple. Some experts propose translating the next clause, 'Has my hour not now come?', which would imply that Mary's petition has initiated the public ministry of Jesus, which is exactly what happens.

So, the mother said to the servants, 'Do whatever he tells you.' Mary doesn't waste words. This is her last recorded utterance: her whole life on earth is summed up in this simple sentence. Mary's existence is for him and relative to him. As the one who pondered God's word in her heart, she lives to welcome his words and to live them out as best she can – she truly is Mother of the Word. Not only because she carried the Father's Son in her womb for nine months, but because she receives his every word, makes it hers, and then offers it to those she meets with every fibre of her being. If we'd been those servants, surely tempted to panic at the crisis, Mary's serene manner would have brought us calm, and her words would have encouraged us resolutely to fulfil the Master's orders.

However, Jesus doesn't seem to get the problem: they need wine, so why fill stone jars with water? The servants, though, don't quibble: they've learnt from Mary to follow out his instructions. And the water became wine – the best wine, kept for the end! We are reminded of Naaman the Syrian (cf. 2 Kings 5) who went to Elisha to be healed of his leprosy. At the prophet's request to simply bathe in the Jordan, he went off in a huff – only to be stopped by his servants, who said, 'If the prophet had asked you to do something difficult, would you not have done it?'

Sometimes God is asking us something very simple but we don't always see the link between our problem and his instructions. Saint Bernadette probably didn't understand why the Lady asked her to dig in the ground at Lourdes, yet she obeyed; gradually, a spring gushed forth, which continues to bring blessings to pilgrims today. The saints are people who obey what God is telling them to do, even if they don't grasp his purpose; when we say 'yes' to his gentle promptings, he can do great things. When we don't feel we can clearly hear what he's asking of us, we can turn to Mary. She always works to help us listen to the words of her Son, and guide us closer to him. Walking on our journey as disciples who follow the Lord, we can become missionaries of his love. God gives generously of his gifts to those who say 'yes' to his will – and through his disciples (with all their faults and failings) he can bring the whole world to discover that his will brings peace and joy.

When all else fails …

Occasionally I used to take the ferry to Clare Island (off Co. Mayo) to celebrate Mass for the small but welcoming parish community there. The first time, my attention was drawn to a notice in the ferry lounge: 'When all else fails, try doing what the captain suggested' – sound advice for the journey, I thought. I easily found the (slightly ancient) car kept for priests visiting the island, with the key in it, and drove off feeling like Jason Bourne. Before long I was lost in the dark, and worse, the car alarm went off – I felt more like Fr Bean at this stage. Fortunately, a kind neighbour came to my rescue and all was well. The friendliness of the islanders and a glorious sunrise the next morning more than made up for my plight. We sometimes feel that every day we fall short of doing his will, but God loves a good trier and will never let us down, if we keep learning to trust on the way.

3. The Proclamation of the Kingdom: Life in the Spirit (Mark 1:14-15)

'After John had been arrested … Jesus proclaimed the Good News from God. "The time has come and the kingdom of God is close at hand."' The Word now speaks, to proclaim the kingdom; he came to set us on fire with God's love, and to lead us to have faith in him. 'Faith comes from what is preached, and what is preached comes from the word of Christ' (Romans 10:17). Jesus never wrote any books (that we know of), he certainly didn't appear on television or have a blog. He spoke, confirming his authority by the

II. When You Walk By the Way

mighty works witnessed by his hearers, and their hearts were opened to listen to him and then to spread the word of the good news that God had come in person to show his friends the way to the Kingdom.

Ask your father and he will tell you

My dad Anthony (1923–2007) liked praying the Rosary; in 1978, he wrote a short article on his own journey with the Rosary, starting in his dry, witty style with the problems involved in reciting it at the wheel (he had a long drive to work every day), wrapping the beads around the wipers, which would suddenly be activated, and so on – until he discovered the finger Rosary. He then went on to propose a new set of Rosary mysteries to complete the traditional Joyful, Sorrowful and Glorious Mysteries. He called them the *Five Mysteries of the Ministry*: (1) The Baptism of Jesus; (2) The Marriage Feast of Cana; (3) The Miracles of Healing; (4) The Transfiguration; (5) The Eucharist.

I don't know if Dad was influenced – even subconsciously – by the writings of Blessed Bartolo Longo, who inspired St John Paul II to add the Mysteries of Light to those recited by the faithful (in his Apostolic Letter *Rosarium Virginis Mariae* of 2002) but his list is startlingly close to that of the late Holy Father! John Paul II's Letter is well worth a read, as is the life story of Blessed Bartolo, whose journey from satanic 'priest' and militant anti-Catholic to Dominican tertiary and fervent apostle of the Rosary would make a great movie. The disciple who has come from a very dark place to encounter God's kindly light is the most powerful witness to his mercy – and can wake us from our apathy to grasp that life's choices matter; the moral decisions we make have eternal consequences.

The third Mystery of Light is different from the nineteen others, each of which commemorates a specific event in salvation history; here we have a kind of summing up of the public ministry of Jesus, focusing on his preaching of the Kingdom – and his call to repentance. With Dad's intuition in mind (the 'miracles of healing,') we can include in our meditation all the saving actions of the Lord: his words, miracles, casting out devils – for 'it was to undo all that the devil has done that the Son of God appeared' (1 John 3:8) – and healings.

We need to talk about … repentance

As we 'walk by the way' on our journey to the Light, we seek to understand what *repentance* means: its original sense is something like 'change your mind' (in Greek) or even better, 'return, come home' (in Hebrew). Both semantic worldviews can help us overcome any negative connotations around the English term. We constantly need to change our minds, bombarded as they are with attitudes and influences contrary to the Spirit: 'Do not model yourselves on the behaviour of the world around you, but let your behaviour change, modelled by your new mind' (Romans 12:2). Like the Prodigal Son (cf. Luke 15) we must regularly come to our senses and return home, running back to our heavenly Father who is waiting for us with open arms and a fatted calf (or an appropriate alternative if we're vegetarian). The path to repentance (a bit like the Rosary itself) is simple yet not always easy for us complicated humans: we have to acknowledge that we cannot do it on our own. We need to go to Jesus, for he is the Way. When he chose the twelve apostles, their first calling was 'to be his companions and to be sent out to preach' (Mark 3:14) – yes, 'with power to cast out devils' (verse fifteen), but before this, before even their preaching mandate, their mission was simply *to be with him*. A companion means someone you share your bread with. Jesus invites us to share his life, enjoying his company – then he will send us out to proclaim his saving love for those he places on our path.

Jesus continually calls out to us, as he did to the disciples in their storm-tossed boat (an image of the Church):

'Courage! It is I! Do not be afraid' (Matthew 14:27). When we entrust ourselves to the power of his Word, we can do the impossible – even walk on water. But like Peter, we forget to keep focused on the Lord. We get distracted by the wind and the waves of our daily lives, and we begin to sink. As Peter did, though, we cry out to him as we're sinking and he comes to rescue us. Then we can be even more effective witnesses to his mercy and power, for we have seen that 'even the winds and the sea obey him' (Matthew 8:27).

A state of journeying

A favourite verse of St Paul states: 'The Kingdom of God does not mean eating or drinking this or that, it means righteousness and peace and joy brought by the Holy Spirit' (Romans 14:17). This means that every time we recite the *Our Father*, praying 'Thy Kingdom come,' we ask God to reign in us and throughout the world; he will be only too happy to send his Spirit so that we can experience this righteousness, peace and joy that Paul refers to. The Catechism states boldly, 'The end-time in which we live is the age of the outpouring of the Spirit' (CCC, 2819). If we don't always experience this peace and joy, we can take heart from another quote from the Catechism: 'The universe was created "in a state of journeying" toward an ultimate perfection yet to be attained, to which God has destined it. We call "divine providence" the dispositions by which God guides his creation toward this perfection' (CCC, 302).

So as the missionaries of God's love that we want to be, it's good to know we're in 'a state of journeying,' like the cosmos. We're not yet the finished article. Sometimes we forget that his power is made perfect in weakness; he gently reminds us through all our limitations that he commands the wind and the waves. He doesn't need 'super-apostles,' just friends who can be with him and proclaim his kindness to others.

Mary also walks with us on this journey; one of her titles is *Queen of Apostles*, because she welcomed the Word, and walks alongside those who seek to offer his word to the world. She accompanies her Son's envoys, encouraging them to claim the power that Jesus wants to bestow upon them, the power of his love which transforms our world into what he wants it to be. Taking our inspiration from Mary's joyful acceptance of God's will, every effort to accomplish what he asks of us will be blessed, causing ripples of love and grace to spread through our fragile society, bringing his healing and peace where most needed.

4. The Transfiguration: The Only Way is Up (Luke 9:28-36)

'As he prayed, the aspect of his face was changed and his clothing became brilliant as lightning.' Jesus went up the mountain – the place where God is encountered in Jewish tradition – taking his closest disciples with him. As is often the case, St Luke's account highlights Jesus at prayer: *as he prayed, the aspect of his face was changed.* This closely mirrors a verse in one of my favourite psalms: 'Look towards him and be radiant; let your faces not be abashed' (Psalms 33:6) – in other words, when we seek the Lord in prayer, his glory shines upon us, inwardly, and we will never go away disappointed if we seek him with sincere hearts, in Jesus' name; we could call it a 'pray as you glow' deal between God and ourselves. The same psalm continues, 'those who seek the Lord lack no blessing' (verse eleven); this brings us back to the question posed in our introduction. If we feel weighed down by our limitations and by all that seems to be lacking in our lives, we just have to seek the Good Shepherd; we shall lack nothing (cf. Psalms 22:1). Jesus showed us the way, and the way is upwards. Blessed Pier-Giorgio Frassati, the young Italian social activist who loved mountaineering, took for his motto, *Verso l'alto* ('Towards the heights'). An English equivalent might be 'onwards and upwards'; when we feel we've hit a brick wall, and there's no way out on any side, our sole remaining option is to look up – where he's waiting for us to turn to him so that he can carry us on eagles' wings to a place of safety (cf. Exodus 19:4).

Moses and Elijah who appeared in glory with Jesus 'were speaking of his passing which he was to accomplish in Jerusalem': the Greek word for 'passing' here is *exodus*, literally 'the way out'. Their presence recalls how God freed his people from slavery in Egypt long ago to bring them to the Promised Land. The two greatest prophets of the Old Testament point toward the sacrifice of the Son of Man who will show us the way out of our messy situation. By his death he sets us free from all that entangles us and will 'pass over' to a new kind of life, gaining us access to the kingdom, which is already in our midst: 'Open to me the gates of holiness: I will enter and give thanks' (Psalms 117:19). As St Patrick climbed a mountain in Mayo (now Croagh Patrick) to watch and pray at its summit for forty days and nights – thus inspiring innumerable pilgrims and seekers to do the same – so all the prophets and saints carve out a way for us on our pilgrimage through life, inviting us in our turn to be a people of prophets, sent to become light for the world.

Saint John Vianney can help us once more; when he was appointed pastor (*curé* in French) of the tiny village of Ars in 1818, he walked from the nearby town, and stopped at the crossroads, unsure which road to take. A young lad indicated the right way. The good Curé thanked him, saying: 'You have shown me the way to Ars, I will show you the way to heaven!' Forty-one years later, this same lad died just a few days after the saint – suggesting that he kept his promise. Good pastors – and all those who allow God's love to guide their steps – can show others the way to heaven: by the example of their holy lives, by their words of preaching, and by their prayers (cf. Preface of Holy Pastors, *Roman Missal*).

Lead, Kindly Light

Our journey in prayer, combined with our desire to be authentic witnesses to God's love, meets with obstacles. Remember when you were a child, happily sleeping in, and Mom or Dad came in and turned on the light? 'Time to get up!' It's so tempting to pull the bedclothes over ourselves and block out the light. Something similar can happen when we come before the Lord in prayer: the light is too much for us, it shines into the dark places of our souls we'd rather avoid bringing to the light. God reveals to us gradually who we are, which can be painful. Didn't Jesus say, 'Everyone who does wrong hates the light and avoids it, for fear his actions should be exposed' (John 3:20)? We have to remember, however, that his light is a kindly light. We can make ours the beautiful prayer of my fellow Londoner, Blessed John Henry Newman: 'Lead, kindly Light, amid the encircling gloom, lead thou me on! The night is dark, and I am far from home, lead thou me on!' Written after he fell gravely ill while travelling, some years before his homecoming to the Catholic Church, this poem helps us to overcome our fears to welcome the light that shines in our darkness. Through it, Newman encourages us to 'sing the praises of God who called you out of the darkness into his wonderful light' (1 Peter 2:9).

A fairly humorous passage in the Old Testament shows us another snare on our *camino*, our journeying to the Promised land. After Moses had gone to the trouble of leading the Israelites out of slavery through the desert, you'd think they would be most grateful to him (and to God). Not so: they begin to wail: 'Who will give us meat to eat? Think of the fish we used to eat free in Egypt, the cucumbers, melons, leeks, onions and garlic!' (Numbers 11:4-5) – I like to add 'and chocolate' when I'm preaching on this passage, to see if anyone is still listening.

As an anonymous wit once remarked, 'Nostalgia ain't what it used to be!'; the chosen people, finding desert life something of a drudge, think back to the wonderful life they had previously, conveniently forgetting that they were slaves. We can do the same: when we feel we're wandering in the wilderness, we can daydream about how much fun we might have had when we could do what we wanted, unencumbered by any pangs of conscience or sense of religious duty – yet we know deep down that only the truth will set us free, that in God alone is our soul at rest (cf. Psalms 61). Once more, those who've come from a long way off proclaim mercy most effectively; a friend who was once a violent criminal now evangelises with a conviction and sense of urgency that most of us don't have. 'Do not behave in the way that you liked to before you learnt the truth … be holy in all you do, since it is the Holy One who has called you' (1 Peter 1:14-15).

The glory of God

'Happy the pure in heart: they shall see God' (Matthew 5:8). As Fr Raniero Cantalamessa once pointed out, the biblical opposite of purity isn't impurity but *hypocrisy*: the pure heart is transparent, there is a harmony between thought, word and deed. How can we obtain this purity? Jesus said in another place, 'If you believe you will see the glory of God' (John 11:40). So faith and purity seem to go together and their goal is beholding God's glory. In Mary, we find the answer: 'Blessed is she who believed' (Luke 1:45). May she help us to grow in faith on our journey up the mountain, and so find harmony within our being, the purity which leads us to the vision of God.

5. The Institution of the Eucharist: You are What You Eat (Luke 22:14-20)

'I have eagerly desired to eat this Passover with you before I suffer.' Jesus celebrates the Passover with his disciples, as every practising Jew did each year – but there is something new which had never been done before. 'On the same night that he was betrayed, the Lord Jesus took some bread, and thanked God for it and broke it, and he said, "This is my body, which is for you: do this as a memorial of me".' (1 Corinthians 11:23-24). Firstly, Jesus gave thanks: this is what *Eucharist* means. His life on earth is a constant hymn of thanks as Son to the Father he loves. Now, he gives thanks in an eminent way through the rites of his people, while fulfilling these rites and raising them up to an entirely new level. Whenever we attend Mass, we are sharing in this thanksgiving that Jesus makes to the Father – gratitude and wonder before the Father's goodness, for creation, for the gift of life, and for us. Maybe we don't always feel in the mood for being thankful, in the midst of heavy burdens or struggles, yet thanksgiving can dispel negativity: we can 'rest' in the heart of the Church, and remember that Jesus offered his life for us; he continues to thank the Father for us, and longs to share our daily lives.

This time of waiting

So, the Passover ritual of sharing bread and wine takes on new meaning; by the power of the Lord's word the bread becomes his body, and the wine his blood. This is an unfathomable mystery, yet accessible to the little children. He is God-with-us, displaying compassion for our broken and fragile condition. He wants not just to be with us but to live *in* us, during this time of waiting which is our pilgrim experience on this earth: 'The Lord is waiting to be gracious to you … happy are all who hope in him' (Isaiah 30:18), who wait for him. To grasp something of the extraordinary gift of the Eucharist, we need to 'activate our longing,' rediscover the desire for eternity written into our very being. Then our waiting and longing for heaven will respond to God's waiting and longing for us to be with him. Through the Eucharistic Lord present in our midst until the end of time in the sacred Host, we can truly begin now an experience of heaven on earth. As St Paul explains, there is an essential link between the Last Supper and the death of Jesus on the Cross: 'until the Lord comes, therefore, every time you eat this bread and drink this cup, you are proclaiming his death' (1 Corinthians 11:26). This means that at every Mass, we celebrate the victory of his triumphant sacrifice of love over death and evil, and anticipate the end of time when all the saints will be together at the wedding banquet of the Kingdom. Vatican II beautifully describes the Eucharist as 'a sacrament of love, a sign of unity, a bond of charity, a paschal banquet in which Christ is eaten, the mind is filled with grace, and a pledge of future glory is given to us' (*Sacrosanctum Concilium*, 47).

If we'd been in the upper room with the disciples, we may not have been able to articulate all that was happening, but we might have sensed that an important stage on our journey to love was being fulfilled.

Sound Effects

When we get to Mass on Sunday (and on weekdays if we can) and receive Holy Communion, many good things are happening, if we're well disposed. As the Catechism explains (1391–98), receiving Jesus increases our union with him – and he is risen – so we can access and anticipate our own bodily resurrection from the dead. The Eucharist strengthens us in our spiritual life. The angel said to Elijah, who was tired and a bit depressed, 'Get up and eat, or the journey will be too long for you' (1 Kings 19:7). He then walked to Mount Horeb, where he had an extraordinary encounter with God. Going to communion preserves us from future sins: the more we are united with Christ, our divine friend, the less we will want to hurt him by turning away from him. The Eucharist makes the Church: 'Since there is one bread, we who are many are one body, for we all share in the one bread' (1 Corinthians 10:17). This reality should give us more fervent longing for the unity of all Christians, inspiring us to pray and work for the day when we may all share in the one Bread and one Cup. Going to Mass also commits us to the poor: 'Whatever you did to one of the least of these my brothers, you did to me' (Matthew 25:40). Many saints underline how the Eucharistic Lord gave them the strength to serve him in the most marginalised of his people. We're called to serve Christ in those we meet each day, whether family members, a difficult boss, the person before us in the supermarket queue, that driver who just took our parking place ... With the help of Jesus in the Eucharist, we can begin to love those to whom we wouldn't naturally be drawn; he wants to love them through us.

Precious Moments

One formula of the Penitential Rite of Mass helps us to consider the Eucharist in three moments of time, which express all its dimensions. It brings us back to the *past*: 'You came to gather the nations into the peace of God's kingdom' – we recall the saving presence of Jesus, who gathers us together to be apostles of peace for the world. It helps us in our *present*: 'You come in word and sacrament to strengthen us in holiness' – he is with us, here and now, empowering us to become what we eat and so allow his light to shine in the darkness. Finally, it points to the *future*: 'You will come in glory with salvation for your people' – he is our food for the journey to the Promised Land. The road seems long, we don't always see the way ahead, but he has gone before us to prepare a place for us and will give us the strength we need to complete our trip.

Victoria Station

It's a short walk of under ten minutes from Victoria Station in London to Westminster Cathedral. The contrast between the turmoil of the noisy city and the quiet before the tabernacle is striking. It's good to go in, bringing our turbulent and distracted hearts to Jesus, who wants to bless us with peace. A similar effect can be found in churches in Dublin, Galway, Paris and in every town. When I studied in Rome, I liked to pray in a small chapel just off a busy square; Mother Teresa asked her nuns to pray in the noisiest part of the city, in order to raise up all the noise, the cries of the poor to Jesus. Whether we're in the city or the countryside, we believe he is there, with his friends. 'The Lord takes delight in his people' (Psalms 149:4) and he protects his loved ones and the world more than we can know. Mary is there too; she is the Mother of the Eucharist, offering herself silently with him, for us and the world. Each time we pray the Hail Mary, we ask our Blessed Mother to pray for us, at two distinct points of our lives: 'now' and 'at the hour of our death.' Every day, the duration between this *now* and our last day on earth is lessening; may her loving presence motivate us to keep going, 'racing for the finish, for the prize to which God calls us upwards to receive in Christ Jesus' (Philippians 3:14).

Conclusion: Let your light shine

The Mysteries of Light have added a new dimension to the practice of the Rosary in the Church. They show us that life is a journey: yes, the road is long, but Christ walks at our side and he is the Way, so we needn't fear getting lost. His sacraments – signs and instruments (or means) of grace for the Christian – bear us up on our toilsome trek. In a certain sense, all that we are as believers takes its origin in Baptism and leads to the Eucharist. Water gave us new life in him, he then turns water into wine to bring joy, and wine into his Blood which saves. 'Everything has to be purified with blood; and if there is no shedding of blood, there is no remission' (i.e. forgiveness of sins, Hebrews 9:22). When we seek him in the sacraments, we begin to grasp how it can be that the one who proclaimed, 'I am the Light of the world' (John 8:12) could also state, 'You are the light of the world' (Matthew 5:14). If we ended up thinking that we were light by ourselves, we would eventually become a black hole – so many gurus and false messiahs in history bear witness to this. If, however, we let him be our light, God can 'enlighten' every sector of society and culture.

I love maps. The advent of online maps and sat navs is very practical, but you can't beat a proper wall map (of the world, Europe, Ireland – I've several, even a jigsaw fridge magnet of central London). But there's one kind you may have seen that's different: those night-time satellite photos of the earth, showing which areas are lit up the most.

Maybe God sees our planet in this way. Wherever he finds friends who welcome his light, they become small gleaming beacons, shining out for a world in pitch blackness, slowly enabling him to turn darkness into light.

III. When You Lie Down

Sickness, Suffering and Death – Sorrowful Mysteries
The Greatest Apostolate of All: Blessed and Broken

1. The Agony in the Garden: Learning to Pray (Mark 14:32-42)

We'd prefer to skip this chapter. Like the times we fast-forward a movie to avoid the unpleasant scenes and reach the happy ending more speedily, we'd rather take the 'ring-road around Calvary' and get to the Resurrection. But we know that without Good Friday – and it *is* good – there's no Easter Sunday. In addition, the saints remind us that to sit with the Lord in his hour of need – what we call 'contemplating the Passion of Christ' – somehow brings consolation to him. Praying the Sorrowful Mysteries also, surely, imparts God's grace to those who are suffering, and strengthens us in times of trial. Scripture reminds us of the positive side of the coin, where we only see the negative: 'you will always have your trials but, when they come, try to treat them as a happy privilege; you understand that your faith is only put to the test to make you patient' (James 1:2-3). Imagine a man who's never suffered, just breezing through life – we wouldn't think them much of a person. Of course, this kind of person doesn't exist; every person has a cross. Some crosses, however, are more hidden than others. Even those for whom everything appears to be going swimmingly have their hour of darkness. What matters is not to look enviously at those who seem more blessed than we are, but to give thanks for what we have and for all we're spared from. 'As long as we have food and clothing, let us be content with that' (1 Timothy 6:8) – and to trust that every event of our lives can bring us closer to the one who went through so much pain for us.

'Stay here while I pray': of course, Jesus prays to the Father throughout his earthly life, but now there is a need to go deeper. This challenges us to learn to pray, as something vital and life-giving. Prayer draws us heavenwards; if you stand in a street looking up at the sky, others will also look up to see what's happening. When we pray, we're looking upwards, in a certain sense, and others will be drawn to pray too. For priests and religious, this is our primary responsibility, before any other good work that we might accomplish. I once read an interview with a famous pianist who was asked by his interviewer, 'You mean you have to practise every single day? You, an accomplished pianist?' He replied, 'If I don't practise for one day, I know it. If I don't practise for two days, the critics know it. And if I don't practise for three days, *everyone* knows it!' There's surely a parallel with prayer in that reply.

'*Abba* – Father' Jesus said. 'Everything is possible for you. Take this cup away from me. But let it be as you, not I, would have it'. Elements of the Lord's Prayer can be noticed in Christ's prayer in the garden: his call to *Abba*, the affectionate name for his heavenly Papa; the aligning of his human will with the will of his Father: thy will be done! His appeal to his sleeping companions, 'You should be awake, and praying not to be put to the test' – echoes the penultimate petition of the *Our Father*: Lead us not into temptation. When we don't know how to pray, reciting the Lord's Prayer is enough, as it contains everything we need. Trying to pray is already praying – and God loves a good trier.

Go and lie down

Paradoxically, learning to pray involves learning to lie down, or letting go. 'Go back and lie down' (1 Samuel 3:5) is one of my favourite Bible verses. Young Samuel is serving the old priest Eli in the sanctuary at Shiloh, where the Ark of the Covenant resided at the time of the Judges. The text states, 'It was rare for the Lord to speak in those days; visions were uncommon'. However, 'the sanctuary lamp had not yet gone out': this reminds us of the light God has placed in the hearts of each of his children, a spark of his burning love that needs to be kindled and kept alight. This lamp may be dimmed by sin, by turning away from God, yet his Spirit constantly seeks to revive it. When the Son of Man comes, 'he will not break the crushed reed, nor put out the smouldering wick' (Matthew 12:20, quoting Isaiah 42:3). This expresses his immense respect for our weakness and his desire to renew us always, for we were made in his image.

The Lord calls Samuel, who replies 'Here I am,' but Samuel thinks it's old Eli calling him. After this happens three times, Eli understands it's the Lord calling, and tells Samuel, 'Go and lie down, and if someone calls, say, "Speak, Lord, your servant is listening."' This is what Samuel does, and the Lord indeed speaks to him. Too often we tend to say, 'Listen Lord, your servant is speaking!' This is also a part of prayer; God delights in listening to us. Yet when we invite him to speak, we discover that he has 'the words of eternal life' (John 6:68), and he can fill our emptiness with the fullness of his love.

'Now the Son of Man is to be betrayed into the hands of sinners.' Jesus knows that his hour has come; he has wrestled, on our behalf, with the human reluctance to suffer and to die. Unlike us, he could walk away or call on legions of angels to fight against his adversaries. Yet, he freely chooses the path that he knows will win life for us.

'The Father loves me, because I lay down my life in order to take it up again. No one takes it from me; I lay it down of my own free will, and as it is in my power to lay it down, so it is in my power to take it up again' (John 10:17-18). Love has impelled him to give his life for the world; love inspires us to give of ourselves for him and for others. When we discover that love is stronger than death, all things are possible. The more we are wounded by life's hurts, the more we can let his love sparkle through us. A Chinese proverb states that a vase that's been broken and glued back together is more beautiful, since the light shines through its cracks – there's something very Christian here. 'We are only the earthenware jars that hold this treasure, to make it clear that such an overwhelming power comes from God and not from us' (2 Corinthians 4:7). In times of darkness, we can access this 'overwhelming power' that comes from the Lord who lived through every pain and every anguish of the human race in some mysterious way, in order to transform it by the power that only he can give.

We know from John's Gospel (19:25-27) that Mary was present at the crucifixion of her Son. She does not appear during his painful journey to Calvary but we can be sure she is there, silently following the Lamb (cf. Revelations 14:4) to the place of sacrifice; she is one with him in love and sorrow. His agony is also hers, for she accompanies him through the darkness. Her constant 'yes' to the Father's will encourages us to remain faithful in our own times of incomprehension in the dark vale. 'At night there are tears, but joy comes with dawn' (Psalms 29:6).

2. The Scourging at the Pillar: Making Sense of Wasted Pain (Luke 23:12-15)

'And though Herod and Pilate had been enemies before, they were reconciled that same day.' This verse calls to mind that old photo of Stalin and Mao, united in public for Stalin's seventieth birthday celebration: friends for political purposes, surrounded by grim faces. True friendship can never be based on expediency or partnership in crime. Pilate must do something to quell the potential riot which is being incited by the chief priests; 'the man has done nothing that deserves death, so I shall have him flogged and then let him go'. The absurdity of violence perpetrated on the innocent, often seemingly at random, is embraced by Jesus for us. The forces of evil are unleashed, apparently without limit. Yet, we can learn even from this: in a kind of 'negative theology', we see that whatever the devil rages against is what is most precious. He inspires those working with the darkness to tear at the Lord's flesh – and it is this flesh, born of a woman, born for us, that saves. Through his victory our flesh is inhabited by the Spirit, something that angels, in all their awesome majesty, can only look upon in wonder. 'They ploughed my back like ploughmen, drawing long furrows. But the Lord who is just has destroyed the yoke of the wicked' (Psalms 128:3-4). Every drop of blood shed by the Son of Man creates wellsprings of new life on earth. Every pain he bore helps us to make sense of all our wasted pain.

'Away with him! Give us Barabbas!' screamed the crowd. But *we are Barabbas*: his very name (Bar-Abba) means 'son of the father'. Each of us is called to be the Father's child through his pure gift. Jesus has taken our place, accepting the punishment we merited by our sins, so that we could be the Father's children. 'Through his wounds you have been healed,' St Peter writes in his first letter, the same Peter who denied his Master and ran away at the first hint of danger: 'Christ suffered for you and left an example for you to follow the way he took' (1 Peter 2:21-24). Peter now believes; he has let Christ look at him and love him and because he knows he has been forgiven, he can forgive himself. Like Fr Henri Nouwen's 'wounded healer,' he can be the shepherd of the flock, precisely because he has made mistakes and accepted his weakness, and welcomed the Lord's mercy. If we're looking for perfect leaders, we're probably in the wrong church! The ordination card of the Swiss theologian, Fr Hans Urs von Balthasar, bore as its inscription just three words: 'Blessed, broken, given.' A shepherd who may feel he has nothing to offer the flock but his own brokenness, accepted in faith, is on the way to becoming a good shepherd: the light of the crucified one can 'shine through the cracks' even more powerfully.

Nuns with tattoos

I know several nuns with tattoos. I must clarify, this isn't a pre-requisite for some avant-garde religious order (though nothing would surprise us these days). We should rejoice that a young woman can encounter Christ and desire to consecrate herself to him with all the baggage of her past life, which may remain visible. The contemporary fashion of tattoos is interesting. In much of Western popular culture, everything is temporary – you throw away whatever you tire of – yet tattoos are unavoidably permanent, only removed at great expense and with some discomfort. But in a way, we all have tattoos: we bear the marks of our past sins, hurts and disappointments, some more hidden than others. However, once we meet Christ, who comes to wipe our tears and heal our hurts, we can give thanks for the negative experiences which have brought us to him. We might struggle to say with St Paul, 'I shall be happy to make my weaknesses my special boast' – but we can listen to the Lord saying to us as he did to Paul, 'My grace is enough for you: my power is at its best in weakness' (2 Corinthians 12:8-9). *My grace is enough for you*: this encourages us to enter into the transforming power of God, who can use even the worst events of life for some good purpose, once we give everything to him.

Mary knows all about hurt. She never sinned, she has no past mistakes to regret, but she knows her radical poverty; she is saved by the Cross of Jesus, just as we are. In some way, her sensitive nature feels every wound inflicted on her Son, because she is so closely united with him. Didn't he take flesh from her very being? Mary is the Mother of Mercy; we tend to think that someone so holy and far from our daily struggles couldn't begin to relate to our wretchedness – yet the opposite is true. Precisely because her heart is drawn to the most fragile of her children, she is closest to those who suffer and those who feel the abyss of their pitiful state. A mother's heart grows in compassion and sorrow the more her child suffers. Mary's heart is sorrowful, yet she continues to believe and hope.

Wonder wall

Sometimes it's good to just sit and watch the world go by. One of my favourite spots in Europe is the harbour in the old town of Dubrovnik, Croatia; on the back wall facing the harbour you can sit for hours and contemplate the magnificent coastal view in the bright sunshine. Tourist boats come and go, people walk by continually; you hear snatches of various languages as you watch God's children enjoying their vacation.

We have already considered how Jesus sees the crowds: he knows each one of us intimately and yearns to be part of our lives, even when we're on holiday! The Father watches the whole of his creation with a loving, eternal look. It's an unfathomable mystery to us how he can be present to the whole universe, from the beginning to the end of time, in one constant gaze (not to mention the angelic realms and so on). What is even more unfathomable, however, is the infinite love and mercy with which he contemplates his creatures, his 'being madly in love' with us humans, as the Church Fathers put it.

What strikes us in contemplating this 'crazy gang' that we call the human race is the extraordinary freedom which God has bestowed upon his children, right from the very beginning. From our limited human perspective, we might think that God, seeing Adam and Eve reaching out to take the fruit, and being aware of the terrible consequences for all their descendants (cf. Genesis 3:6), would surely have been anxious to stop them immediately: 'I wouldn't do that if I were you!' But the Father has other ideas: 'my thoughts are not your thoughts, my ways not your ways' (Isaiah 55:8). God, who cannot conceive evil, somehow permits us to make free choices in life each day and doesn't stop loving us despite the wrong choices we sometimes make. However, every choice for the good and the true enables us to become free, to become more of what we're called to be. Before the foundation of the world, the Father chose us in his Son (cf. Ephesians 1:3), knowing that his Son would take upon himself the punishment for our sins. When we sit and enjoy the beauty of creation, or look upon crowds of people, each one invited to walk on this path to true freedom, we can give thanks for the Father's tender look of unfailing love and for the pain that Jesus went through in order to set us free. 'Through his wounds you have been healed' (1 Peter 2:24).

3. The Crowning with Thorns: Behold Your King (Matthew 27:27-31)

'Having twisted some thorns into a crown, they put this on his head and placed a reed in his right hand.' The soldiers are only doing their job, following orders. The tedium of their unpleasant work can be relieved by a bit of sport, poking fun at the most unfortunate of the condemned. 'Father, forgive them; they do not know what they are doing' (Luke 23:34). The downward spiral of violence and contempt seems unstoppable. What could break this vicious circle of hate and cruelty? Only the meekness of the Lamb: 'when he was tortured he made no threats but he put his trust in the righteous judge' (1 Peter 2:23). The irony of the pagan cohort mocking the Lord, saying 'Hail, king of the Jews' is almost too much to bear, even for us with our hearts hardened by the violence we witness so often through movies and news broadcasts. Jesus is the King of kings, he is Lord and Master, yet he reveals his almighty power most of all by his compassion and forgiveness. This is weakness, as the world sees it, yet 'God's' foolishness is wiser than human wisdom, and God's weakness is stronger than human strength' (1 Corinthians 1:25).

Every word, gesture, action or silence of the incarnate Word is a sign, a message from the Father to show us how much he loves us. The subjects of the Roman Empire were used to their leaders proclaiming themselves lord and master, even claiming to be divine. However, the way God chooses to show his authority and power is quite the opposite: we fail to understand why a God, who is good, allows suffering in our world – a common obstacle for non-believers to accept his existence. It is possibly even more difficult to grasp why the infinite, eternal Creator of all things would wish to become one of us, suffer and die for us. Yet, this should impel us to appreciate the infinite worth of each human being and the extraordinary value of life: we are worth it because he showed us so. In addition, the way of the Cross speaks to us as to what kind of God is our God: if he loves us this much, then our only response can be to strive to love him in return. *Gratitude* may be an old-fashioned word, but its sentiment is everlasting. We can never be outdone in generosity by the one who has given us all things, as a free gift. The thorns of our King's crown call us to let go of our pride, to remember that we are not God – yet we are called and chosen to be divine. Church history shows that when we try to be big and powerful, triumphalist even, God's gentle love is obscured and buried. However, when we at least make a start in following our Saviour's way – through the darkness of self-giving love, patience and meekness – then the Church can reveal God's beauty and power to us. Not many followed Jesus on that dark Friday; the large crowds who acclaimed him into Jerusalem with palms only a few days previously had faded away. Yet the message of the Cross reminds us, in the words of St Francis, that 'it is in dying that we are reborn to eternal life'. Possibly the Church has to 'die' in a certain sense – in order to be reborn; this is not the same as withering away, but a letting go of human perspectives of power and control, to focus on what really matters: how Jesus brought victory through defeat, life through death, and meaning through what seems senseless.

The thorn in the flesh

'Father, I used to be able to pray so much, but now I'm

ill, I can't pray any more' – priests often hear this kind of statement. We might know, in theory, that Christ is present in the sick in a particularly powerful way, that there is no need, even, for the sick person to pray, because the Holy Spirit is praying within them. One can't, however, glibly explain a theological concept when faced with someone who is suffering. All one can do is try to reassure them that God is at work, for he never abandons his faithful. But sickness and other trials can dampen the zeal of those who want to serve the Lord with generous hearts. We're tempted to say, 'if only God would remove this problem I have, I'd be able to spread the Gospel more effectively!' What is there to do? As with every profound question of life, the only answer is to look at Jesus, and we see how he saved the world. Yes, he undertook three years of intensive ministry, healing the sick, casting out demons and preaching the Gospel of the kingdom. However, these three years were preceded – prepared for – by thirty years of quiet service and loving community life with Mary and Joseph (what is called the Hidden Life of Christ). Then, his public ministry culminates in this way of the Cross. So, we could say that pains and trials – and anything that we feel is a limitation in our lives, all that prevents us from being the apostles we'd like to be – are in fact the greatest apostolate of all: because now we are letting him do the work. Saint Paul wrote, 'To stop me from getting too proud, I was given a thorn in the flesh' (2 Corinthians 12:7), just after describing the extraordinary revelations he had received from the Lord, having being brought up into 'the third heaven'. We don't know what exactly was troubling Paul; in a way, it's better we don't know, since we can apply his experience of limitation to whatever appears to hamper our willing efforts to serve the Lord. Once again, the best response is that of the Lord himself: 'My grace is enough for you'.

No place like home

You know the feeling: wanting to pack it all in and start afresh somewhere else, leaving all your troubles behind. Around 1981, a British husband and wife decided to do just that: there were riots in England, social tensions were high and the economy was stagnant. So, this professional couple hired management consultants to find the safest place in the world to live, saying, 'Whatever spot the experts come up with, we'll go and settle there'. After extensive research, the consultants concluded that the safest place in the world was … the Falkland Islands (Malvinas) in the South Atlantic. Our happy couple moved there, and (you guessed it) just a few months later, the Argentinian army invaded the islands. There must be a lesson here; we can waste a good deal of energy wishing our lives away, dreaming of utopia. But *utopia* literally means 'no place'! Gazing upon Jesus, who didn't run away but embraced his cross, helps us to accept the limits of our situation. Rather than looking around to a different place where we'd surely find contentment, we can, with his help, be 'at home' right where we are, knowing that he has placed us here for a reason, and that his strength will enable us to find peace in even the most challenging of life's experiences. 'There is nothing I cannot master with the help of the One who gives me strength' says St Paul (Philippians 4:13). Finally, we have to accept the paradoxes of life as opportunities to grow in trust on our walk through 'the valley of darkness' (Psalms 22:4); we don't always know where we're going but the Good Shepherd is there, with crook and staff, encouraging us to believe that our road leads to a better place. 'You have never gone this way before,' said the Lord, as he led the Israelites to the Promised Land (Joshua 3:4). For all the new challenges of our lives and the times we feel we can't cope, he is there and he will never let us down.

4. The Carrying of the Cross: Out of the City (John 19:17-22)

'They then took charge of Jesus, and carrying his own cross he went out of the city to the place of the skull'. It is time to tread the path of the *Via Dolorosa*, the path of sorrows, by which the Lord's Anointed must leave the holy city of Jerusalem, in order to complete the work, he has been given by his Father. Jesus said, 'If anyone wants to be a follower of mine, let him renounce himself and take up his cross and follow me' (Mark 8:34). Following him means leaving our comfort zone, letting go of everything that does not lead to true life, in order to find what really matters. Only love can do this; since he walked this way out of love for us, we know deep down that we can learn to love by following him. Saint Francis de Sales stated, 'Father, in your will is our peace' (a motto which inspired, among others, St John XXIII). When we embrace the will of the one who wants to give us everything, we can truly be free. Despite the weight of the heavy cross, Jesus is somehow at peace, joyfully renewing his 'yes' to the Father's will. Mary, too, is at peace, while at the same time being overwhelmed by sorrow. She knows that the Lamb's sacrifice will bring salvation to a great number of brothers and sisters; she shares his pain and offers herself in union with him. The cross is heavy, the soldiers are impatient: three times the Lord and Master of all things falls to the ground. Yet out of love for us, he must get up again: the Scriptures have to be fulfilled, the work for which he came into this world must be accomplished. Without love, suffering is meaningless and absurd. But love grows through pain; Jesus, consoled by the silent presence of Mary somewhere in that raucous crowd, and by the small group of faithful followers, reaches that place of sacrifice where he, the high priest himself, will be the altar and victim.

The Great Week

Holy Week (called the 'Great Week' in Irish) is the highlight of the Church's liturgical year, featuring a generous selection of Scripture readings to help us focus on the key events of salvation history. Tucked away almost unnoticed, in the first Gospel of Palm Sunday is a phrase of Jesus' which brings meaning to every aspect of our lives. When Jesus sends two disciples to go and fetch the tethered colt upon which he will ride into Jerusalem, he instructs them with what to say if anyone asks them what they're doing: 'The Master needs it' (Mark 11:3). These four words can provide a response to every 'why' of the human race. Whatever our pain and negative experiences, whatever the absurdity of all that we don't understand, the contradictions and bewildering turns of life and our shattered dreams, once we can begin to believe that *the Master needs it*, we're already looking at our messy situation in a new light. Even to grasp that the Lord of the cosmos chooses to *need* something from me is liberating. 'Remember how generous the Lord Jesus was: he was rich, but he became poor for your sake, to make you rich out of his poverty' (2 Corinthians 8:9). Previous generations were used to stating 'offer it up' when things went wrong; these days, this attitude can appear somewhat masochistic. God doesn't want us to suffer for the sake of it. Nevertheless, once we turn it over to his mercy, he can make use of every ache and pain, and every wrong turn.

Little Sparrow

We nowadays tend to downplay sin, preferring not to think too much about negative things. But the violent reality of the cross breaks through our complacency to grasp what sin really is and what it cost to transform us into an offering pleasing to God. Yet through his sacrifice, we are truly set free. All he wants is the smallest bit of love in our hearts that we can give him, the merest gesture of thanksgiving and trust, to wash our stains away and enable us to walk freely, 'ransomed, healed, restored, forgiven' as the old hymn proclaims.

I was once with a group of friends stopping for petrol; there, in the garage forecourt, was a tiny sparrow, hopping piteously. A closer look revealed what was wrong: the poor creature had trodden in some chewing-gum. Unable to extricate itself, it struggled to break free. Each of us tried to approach the little bird to remove its burden so that it could fly away, but it was too frightened to let anyone near. This can be a parable for what sin does to us: it ensnares us, weighing us down, and we hide – like Adam and Eve in the garden – to avoid facing the Liberator, who only wants to remove our chewing-gum and let us fly to the heights. Even our worries and cares can become like a ball and chain preventing us from running freely; that is why we need to go to him to follow in his steps. Sometimes the road seems to lead to a dead end, but he will always find an *exodus*, a way out for us. 'Unload all your worries on to him, since he is looking after you' (1 Peter 5:7).

The best Stations ever

Pilgrims to various shrines have, on occasion, had to endure my meditations for the Way of the Cross. One particular group visiting a Marian shrine in Central Europe seemed happy enough for me to lead them in the traditional fourteen Stations. I was well prepared, armed with a handy booklet of meditations and Scripture quotes; they were going to love this! The first drop of rain fell at around the second station. By the fifth, it was a torrential downpour. I naturally expected the group to run for cover, as all the other pilgrims already had. But these were hardy souls from Reunion Island (in the Indian Ocean), they weren't going to let a bit of mild drizzle interrupt their prayer time. We plodded on, soaked to the skin. The noise of the rain made it impossible to speak or even shout – no one would have heard anyway. At each station, we simply stood in silence for a short while, dripping buckets. They seemed to be praying intensely; I was praying it would soon be over. There comes a point when you don't even feel bothered by the rain, you can't possibly get any wetter than you are – somehow a different kind of prayer was being initiated. At last it was over, and we headed for the guesthouse and a hot shower. But I'd realised something: it was the most moving and memorable *Via Crucis* I'd ever 'conducted'. Because we (well, I) had let go of our own plan, our own way of meditating, in order to let the Lord speak to us in a way we hadn't anticipated at all. 'Showers and rain, all bless the Lord! Give glory and eternal praise to him' (Daniel 3:64). The God of surprises speaks powerfully to us when we let him – even if sometimes the elements must reduce us to a mute state, despite our own ideas. 'It is good to wait in silence for the Lord to save' (Lamentations 3:25).

5. The Crucifixion: Into Your Hands (Luke 23:33-46)

Jesus said, 'Father, forgive them; they do not know what they are doing'. It is the hour of darkness, for the one who came to bring life is put to death. Because of envy, religious fanaticism and political expediency, this inconvenient prophet has been hastily eliminated after the feeblest attempt at a show trial. He stands there, in the name of all the innocent ones, all the falsely accused victims throughout history, as the bridge between heaven and earth, and the gateway to the Father's house. Even on the cross, his main desire is to forgive, pleading with his Father to show mercy to those who are unaware of the enormity of their actions. 'They do not know what they are doing.' They are indeed cruelly torturing an innocent man, but how can they see that this is the Son of man, the incarnate Word who came to give his life for all people of all time? Even Caiaphas had pronounced on the Lord's fate, yet remained seemingly ignorant of the weight of his words: 'it was as high priest that he made this prophecy that Jesus was to die for the nation – and not for the nation only, but to gather together in unity the scattered children of God' (John 11:51-52). Jesus came to *gather* a divided world into unity; all those who follow him can find wholeness since he gathers the scattered fragments of our lives and makes them into something beautiful.

Jesus had stated before Pilate, 'Mine is not a kingdom of this world; I was born for this, I came into the world for this: to bear witness to the truth' (John 18:36-37). Now he gives the ultimate witness to the truth about the destructive nature of sin – for he is the Lamb who takes upon himself the sins of the world. Even more fully, however, he reveals the truth about God's love for the world; he himself is the Truth, his whole being manifests the Father's burning desire for each one of us to know his love. Saint John Paul II once wrote, in reference to the patron and martyr of Poland, St Stanislaus, 'If the word will not convert, blood will convert'. When words are not enough, we can welcome the Blood poured out for us, to soften our hearts and bring us new life. This routine execution on a dark afternoon by uninterested Roman soldiers, in the presence of the smug chief priests, was only witnessed by a handful of followers. Most of the disciples had run away. The glory of the Son of God was veiled, his beauty disfigured by the callous treatment of his oppressors. He truly was 'a man of sorrows and familiar with suffering, a man to make people screen their faces; he was despised and we took no account of him' (Isaiah 53:3).

When we read certain passages of the Old Testament in the light of the New – as Christians have been doing ever since the Holy Spirit came at Pentecost, particularly in the liturgy – we are struck by how closely they correspond to the suffering of the Christ: the Servant Songs in Isaiah (especially 52-53, read during the Celebration of the Passion on Good Friday), the Just One of the book of Wisdom (chapter three) – probably the last book of the First Covenant to be written, around 50BC – and in particular Psalm 21. The latter is recited by Jesus himself on the Cross: 'My God, my God, why have you forsaken me?' – yet concludes in a triumphant tone of praise and thanksgiving. Here, Jesus does not address God as *Abba*, Father; it is as though he is deprived even of the awareness that he'd enjoyed throughout his earthly life of his unique relationship with the Father as the beloved Son. He thus unites himself to all the afflicted and abandoned of our world, along with all those who do not know that God is their Father or that they are loved by him. But was Jesus also dropping a hint to the religious authorities who had condemned him? Would any of them go home and read this psalm, seeing in it the journey of the oppressed one from torture to victory through the goodness of God? 'You are my praise in the great assembly … the poor shall eat and shall have their fill … all the earth shall remember and return to the Lord … These things the Lord has done'!

There are apparently two words in Hebrew for 'why': *madoua* is causal, referring to the past: why did this happen to me? The biblical term *lama*, however, turns to the future, implying 'wherefore': what is the purpose of this? We see this distinction in the cure of the man born blind. The disciples seek the cause of his affliction: 'Who sinned, this man or his parents?' Jesus, however, points to a future purpose: 'He was born blind so that the works of God might be displayed in him' (John 9:2-3). So, when we're undergoing trials, we can certainly cry out to God, 'why have you abandoned me?' It helps, however, to look for purpose: there is a reason for everything, a final answer to all our questions. Once again, the Master needs it – and he sees the bigger picture. 'What we suffer in this life can never be compared to the glory, as yet unrevealed, which is waiting for us' (Romans 8:18).

Rest in peace

Among the final few words of Jesus on the Cross, we find another near-quotation of a psalm: 'Father, into your hands I commend my spirit' (Luke 23:46 and Psalms 30:6) – but Jesus says *Father* instead of *Lord* (which we find in the psalm) as if to celebrate his unique relationship with the invisible God. In addition, it's as though he is inviting us to call God *Father*, since we will be adopted as his children, through the very sacrifice of Christ on the Cross. So, the Son gives up his Spirit in his final saving action on this earth, and our redemption is assured. The Letter to the Hebrews underlines his death as *rest* – echoed in the tradition of saying 'rest in peace' when a loved one dies. Hadn't Jesus himself said, 'Come to me, and I will give you rest' (Matthew 11:28)? How can we reach the place of rest he has promised (cf. Hebrews 4:1), even now, during our daily struggle? How can we find repose and serenity in our fragmented and noisy society?

Recently, I came across an article online, entitled 'Ten Tips for People Who Are Tired All the Time'. Most of the suggestions were a trifle obvious (sleep more, drink more water) – but the last one caught my attention: 'Avoid toxic people'. Most of us would reply, 'I wish I could!' and think no more of it. Jesus, however, didn't avoid toxic people: he came to eat with sinners. I think if we met Jesus, we would find him the most restful, serene person we'd ever encountered. What was his secret? 'In God alone is my soul at rest' (Psalms 61:2). Jesus doesn't simply commend his spirit to the Father at the last moment of his earthly life. From his earliest days among us, he had rendered his being to the Father's tender care, finding his rest in God alone, and thus showed us the way to do the same. His final words on earth are 'It is accomplished' (John 19:30) – he has won the victory! Hell is vanquished and we can triumph over all our trials, witnessing that the Cross is strength and weakness is power if we strive to live with him and in him. Then we will truly find rest in the Father's hand.

Conclusion: Await the Dawn

'Near the cross of Jesus stood his mother ... Seeing his mother and the disciple he loved standing near her, Jesus said to his mother, 'Woman, this is your son'. Then to the disciple he said, 'This is your mother'. And from that moment, the disciple made a place for her in his home' (John 19:25-27).

Mary stands by the cross of Jesus watching his fate; we can scarcely imagine her pain, yet we are glad that she is there. She will always be there at the side of her children who suffer, standing in faith – because God's love has triumphed – and waiting in hope, since the one who promised new life is faithful; he always keeps his promises. Jesus' parting gift to us is his own mother; by entrusting her to the beloved disciple, he gives her to each one of us, for every single one of us is his dear friend and beloved disciple. As we learn to 'lie down,' to let go of our own ways – and even of our most religious plans and all we'd like to do for the Lord, which is still too much *our* will – she will constantly be at our side to await the dawn of the new times. Her quiet presence gives us a glimpse of the fulfilment, when our world will finally be what God wants it to be, a place of light and love, joy and laughter; the kingdom of God is very near.

'Remember, O most gracious Virgin Mary, that never was it known that anyone who fled to your protection, implored your help or sought your intercession, was left unaided. Inspired with this confidence, I fly to you, O Virgin of virgins, my Mother; to you do I come, before you I stand, sinful and sorrowful. O Mother of the Word Incarnate, despise not my petitions, but in your mercy, hear and answer me. Amen'.

IV. And When You Rise

The Life of Heaven – Glorious Mysteries
Toward the Goal: Their Fruits Go Before Them

1. The Resurrection: New Life (Luke 24:1-12)

'Why look among the dead for someone who is alive?' He is Risen! The darkness of Good Friday, when Life was put to death and darkness prevailed over the whole land, is now transformed by some process which we can't begin to explain – through an event seen by the angels of heaven and possibly by the just of the underworld waiting to rise, but which apparently had no human witness on this earth. Jesus has been raised in bodily form by the power of the Father, through the agency of the life-giving Spirit. This central event of human history is shrouded in mystery, yet will become the core of the Church's proclamation until the end of time: 'You killed him, but God raised him to life, freeing him from the pangs of Hades … God raised this man Jesus to life, and all of us are witnesses to that' (Acts 2:23-24, 32). Such is the forceful message of St Peter, empowered by the Spirit to preach on the day of Pentecost, a message which must be proclaimed in every generation, until the Lord comes in glory!

'Having risen in the morning on the first day of the week, he appeared first to Mary of Magdala' (Mark 16:9) – we might object that Jesus surely would have appeared first of all to his Mother Mary, who was closer to him than any other believer? This is a tradition strongly present in the Eastern Churches, and is also posited in the writings of St Ambrose and St Ignatius of Loyola, as well as by St John Paul II. A stained-glass window in St Mary's Parish Church of Fairford, Gloucestershire also celebrates the imagined meeting of the Risen Jesus and his Mother. So, without discounting the likelihood of Jesus manifesting himself to his Mother in some way, we can understand the apparition to Mary Magdalene – 'from whom he had cast out seven devils' – as underlining the infinite mercy of the Saviour and his delight in rewarding those who seek him with love. 'Anybody who loves me will be loved by my Father, and I shall love him and show myself to him' (John 14:21). A central feature of the resurrection accounts in the gospels is the *encounter*: Jesus meets Mary Magdalene, then the two disciples on the road to Emmaus, the eleven apostles and 'more than five hundred of the brothers at the same time' (1 Corinthians 15:6). Each one of these would have told the story for the rest of their lives; we may feel far away historically from them, but in the communion of saints, we're all one family. The Risen Lord continues to bring his friends together, sometimes in the most unexpected of ways. With Jesus, every encounter leads to a new mission: when we come across him, everything is changed. We might prefer to plod on as before, minding our own business, yet as Peter and John stated fearlessly to the Sanhedrin, 'we cannot promise to stop proclaiming what we have seen and heard' (Acts 4:20). We see how Jesus gives a mandate to those to whom he appears: 'Go and find the brothers and tell them: I am ascending to my Father and your Father, to my God and your God' (John 20:17).

'God-incidences'

When I lived in Ireland, I regularly drove through the village of Shrule in Co. Mayo, where the Society of St

Columban was founded in 1918, with a Church mandate to send missionaries to China. Some years ago in Knock, I met a young man from a city in central China. He had recently become a Catholic, crediting a Columban sister as instrumental in his journey to the faith. In God's plan, the boldness of a small group of fervent disciples in a village of Mayo had eventually led to a Chinese boy encountering Christ, then coming all the way back to Mayo to complete the circle. At random, I mentioned that my friend Declan from Galway (now a priest) had once spent a year in China. His face lit up: 'Oh yes, Declan, he stayed in my house!' Indeed he had. What are the odds? Jungian psychologists speak of *synchronicity*, which holds that events are 'meaningful coincidences' if they occur with no causal relationship yet seem to be related. The Christian, however, would see, in these events, divine Providence in action: the Father is ever at work to guide circumstances to further his plans of salvation. I like to call these events 'God-incidences'; Jesus has many friends in different places, and he loves for his friends to meet one another. Every new friendship, willed by Providence, can impart encouragement to each of us on our journey and further the mission of the whole Church.

'There is no God'

I once heard a talk by a priest who began by announcing solemnly with a deadpan expression, 'There is no God: it's written in the Bible!' Once he'd got his listeners' attention, he explained that the passage from the Psalms states, 'The fool has said in his heart: "There is no God above"' (Psalms 13:1 and 52:2). His point was to warn against taking Scripture passages out of context; we can take verses in isolation – as the devil does when tempting Jesus in the wilderness, quoting a psalm to justify his suggestion (Matthew 4:6). The Church encourages us to interpret Scripture as a totality, 'according to the whole', which is the literal meaning of the word 'catholic' in Greek. A 'fool,' in biblical language, is someone who acts as if God didn't exist. We can all be foolish sometimes. When the weather is grey and foggy, with no sign of the sun, you have to keep believing that the sun is up there – somewhere. I imagine a little hobbit-like creature coming out of his hole: if I met him on a dull day, would I be able to convince him that the sun exists? 'It's up there, you just have to take my word for it!' Of course, when the sun finally appears the countryside is transformed, the earth is bathed in light and its beauty shines out. And so it is with God: we can't see him yet we believe he's 'up there somewhere' and we may try to convince doubters he exists ... but when we pray, everything changes!

Tea in the Sahara

Being a coffee aficionado, I never drink tea. Sometimes, however, you cannot refuse: I once found myself sitting in the tent of a semi-nomadic Bedouin in the Sahara Desert. Tea was served, the kind of situation where it would be churlish to decline; that was the last time I drank tea. Now I'm not sure how I'd have reacted if I'd been there on the lakeside when Jesus offered some grilled fish to his friends saying, 'Come and have breakfast' (John 21:12). Grilled fish for breakfast? Give me coffee and toast any time. But when it's Jesus himself who makes you breakfast, you'd have to reconsider. *Come and have breakfast*: there's something supremely ordinary about this invitation. After a fruitless night's fishing, Peter and his companions are guided to catch a large quantity of fish by the mysterious stranger on the shore – then he cooks them breakfast! The Lord sees our (apparently) fruitless days and nights, our wasted time; once we desire to serve him, nothing is wasted in his eyes. When we bring him our empty nets, he can fill them by his power. When we find that all is darkness and grief, we must simply open our hearts to his risen presence so that he can shine his light and joy upon us. 'If one of you hears me calling and opens the door, I will come in to share his meal, side by side with him' (Apocalypse 3:20).

2. The Ascension: Learning to Hope (Luke 24:50-53)

'As he blessed them, he withdrew from them and was carried up to heaven'. After forty days of appearing to his friends, Jesus now leaves them as he had said he would. 'It is good for you that I go' (John 16:7): in order to send us the Holy Spirit, Jesus returns to the Father. Since he is the Way, we must then hope that every time we go to the Father in prayer, in the name of Jesus, the Father can send the Spirit of his Son upon us and the world. This mystery might seem, at first glance, to highlight the Lord's *absence*: wouldn't we be sad if Jesus left us? Yet his disciples 'went back to Jerusalem full of joy' – since he went before them to prepare a place for them, and the promised Spirit would remind them of all he had told them, not least his parting words in Matthew's Gospel: 'Know that I am with you always; yes, to the end of time' (28:20). This mystery can help those grieving loved ones who've left us for heaven, for they, in a different way, can be closer to us now than they were on earth. Mary helps us see the big picture; even though her Son has gone, she no longer grieves. As she lived in such closeness to him in faith and love, she can inspire us to be joyful even when God no longer seems present. She was certainly there for the apostles during those days of waiting for the Spirit; her joy and calmness surely enabled these men to wait in hope. 'Blessed is she who believed' (Luke 1:45), and blessed are we when we ask her to help us to live in faith, by which the Lord's apparent absence is turned into presence.

Pixel Deficiency

Have you ever had that sense of annoyance when you have a mark on your computer screen? This happened to me while writing this book: no amount of rubbing or scratching the screen could remove it, an irritating distraction caused by such a tiny spot! The PC repair man explained that my laptop was suffering from pixel deficiency: the mark was a missing pixel beneath the screen and replacing it would be expensive. An external monitor solved the problem, but it got me thinking. The giant mosaic in Knock Basilica, depicting the apparition of 1879, is made up of some 1.5 million pieces of coloured glass (so we're told, I've never counted them). If just one of those small squares had been mislaid in transit, this magnificent work of art would be incomplete, lacking something. This reminds us of how precious we are in God's eyes, since there would be something missing in his plan if one of us wasn't there. As Pope Benedict said at his inauguration Mass in 2005, 'Only when we meet the living God in Christ do we know what life is. We are not some casual and meaningless product of evolution. Each of us is the result of a thought of God. Each of us is willed, each of us is loved, each of us is necessary.' Benedict would certainly be familiar with the writings of Blessed John Henry Newman, who once wrote: 'God has created me to do him some definite service. He has committed some work to me which he has not committed to another. I have my mission. I may never know it in this life, but I shall be told it in the next. I am a link in a chain, a bond of connection between persons. He has not created me for naught. I shall do good; I shall do his work.'

So, what are we to do? We can relate to those who asked Jesus, 'What must we do if we are to do the works that God wants'? The reply he gave was, 'This is working for God: you must believe in the one he has sent' (John 6:28-29). In the original Greek text, there is a strong distinction between the term used by his followers – the *works* (plural) of God – and his answer – the *work* (singular) of God – which is sometimes lost in translation. There's a world of difference! We can strive to do good works for God, but when wanting to be in charge of our own plans, we can end up thinking our efforts are what get us into heaven instead of the grace of God who invites us to cooperate with him. We can even seek to control our prayer life: saying the Rosary is good (I'm sure you'll agree, if you've read this far), so we might think that reciting four sets of rosaries must be even better – but only if it's what he wants us to do. *The work of God is to believe in the one he has sent*: when we live in faith, we recall that it is his work. Then, praying one *Our Father* with ardent devotion might have more merit than a whole Rosary said mechanically; as St Paul wrote, 'what matters is faith that makes its power felt through love' (Galatians 5:6).

Take the Elevator

I'm not one for interpreting dreams, but when a young friend asked what could the meaning of her dream be about being in a lift, I thought immediately of St Thérèse of Lisieux. Thérèse discovered early on in religious life that she wasn't able to live like the great saints; she compared her 'little way' with taking the lift instead of the stairs: 'I wish to find an elevator which would raise me to Jesus, for I am too small to climb the rough stairway of perfection. The elevator which must raise me to heaven is your arms, O Jesus!' She first saw a lift in a hotel in Paris that she stayed in with her sister Céline, when their father Louis took them on pilgrimage to Rome. It's well known that Friedrich Nietzsche, the German philosopher and atheist, often stayed in the same hotel; various authors have imagined how a conversation between them might have gone. (The late Archbishop of Paris, Cardinal Lustiger, once attended as a young student the same classes at the Sorbonne as Pol Pot, who would become the ruthless leader of Cambodia; how different the history of that country might have been if the latter had listened to Lustiger's energetic proclamation of the Gospel.)

Thérèse's 'little way' is all about trust. She inspires us to take the elevator; if we feel too small to reach heaven by our own efforts, we can let the Father raise us up to the heights. On the subject of dreams, a nurse I know was caring for a young boy with special needs confined to a wheelchair; one night, not so long ago, she dreamt he was walking and even dancing joyfully. The next day at work, she was told that he'd died the previous evening. Was her dream a glimpse from the Lord of the new life he now enjoyed in heaven? I like to think so. The God who can turn our dreams into plans calls us, above all, to have faith and trust in him, in order to bring us up where we belong; the poor, the sick and the little ones show us the way. As G. K. Chesterton wrote, 'Humility is the mother of giants. One sees great things from the valley; only small things from the peak'.

3. Pentecost: Receive the Holy Spirit
   (Acts 2:1-4)

'They were all filled with the Holy Spirit, and began to speak foreign languages, as the Spirit gave them the gift of speech'. We know from the first chapter of the Acts of the Apostles that the Twelve (now brought back to their original number by the inclusion of Matthias, who took Judas Iscariot's place) went back to Jerusalem after watching Jesus ascend into heaven. They went to the 'upper room' – probably the same room in which they had celebrated the Last Supper with the Master. For nine days, they 'joined in continuous prayer, together with several women, including Mary the mother of Jesus, and with his brothers' (Acts 1:14). This first Novena is our template for the Church at prayer: when we strive to pray continuously, united with the Apostles and with Mary, the mother of Jesus – without necessarily knowing what to pray for, or what's going to happen – the Holy Spirit can work wonders. 'The Spirit too comes to help us in our weakness. For when we cannot choose words in order to pray properly, the Spirit himself expresses our plea in a way that could never be put into words' (Romans 8:26). It's good to recall that the Apostles were beset with flaws, fears and even doubts (cf. Luke 24:38); they didn't have all the answers and could scarcely imagine what God was going to do next. If we come to prayer with our certainties and set plans all laid out it's hard for the Spirit to break through – but when we bring our fears and brokenness before him, he can 'pick up the pieces' (John 6:12) and transform our lives. If we 'watch with Mother' we are stronger; Mary's presence magnifies the gifts of the Spirit for her children, and her faith and hope – which she no longer has need of in Paradise – are at our disposal, to help us truly live in the Spirit. Thus, we can respond to St Paul's wonderful prayer: 'May he give you the power through his Spirit for your hidden self to grow strong, so that Christ may live in your hearts through faith … until, knowing the love of Christ, which is beyond all knowledge, you are filled with the utter fullness of God' (Ephesians 3:16-19).

So, the Holy Spirit comes on the tenth day: he appears as a mighty wind and as tongues of fire, enabling these weak, timid men to go out boldly into the streets of Jerusalem to proclaim the Good News of Jesus. 'Now raised to the heights by God's right hand, he has received from the Father the Holy Spirit, who was promised, and what you see and hear is the outpouring of that Spirit' (Acts 2:33). Each of their listeners, gathered from 'every nation under heaven' (Acts 2:5) heard the apostles speaking in their own language. The Spirit brings fire, energy and understanding; the power of the Risen One, now ascended to the Father, collaborates with the good will of his friends, to launch the worldwide mission of the Church. He had commanded them, 'Go out to the whole world; proclaim the Good News to all creation' (Mark 16:15) – something which must have seemed absurd, utterly impossible for this small, shy group of disciples. But with God, all things are possible! Only with his Spirit can we receive the strength to spread the Word, yet with his help we can do all that he asks of us.

Many Tongues

It's thought there are currently some seven thousand languages in the world, many of which are threatened with extinction. I have an old book, 'The Gospel in Many Tongues' by the British and Foreign Bible Society, which lists one verse (usually John 3:16: 'God so loved the world …') in eight hundred and seventy-five languages, most of which I've never even heard of; may God reward those Christian missionaries who toiled to bring His word to the very ends of the earth! Curiously, there's one important language missing from it: Aramaic, the mother tongue of Jesus himself. Another kind of language isn't there, but one wouldn't expect it in a reference book of this kind: sign languages used by deaf people. Every time I witness their gestures in the liturgy, I feel uplifted. Their rendering of the *Our Father* is particularly poignant, a wordless body-prayer in unison which could leave no onlooker unmoved. As St John writes of his vision in the Apocalypse, 'I saw a huge number, impossible to count, of people from every nation, race, tribe and language' (7:9). In heaven, the saints sing in harmony, filled with the Spirit who unites them into one people, praising God eternally in one tongue, the language of love.

Counting Sheep

Jesus affirmed before Pilate, 'All who are on the side of truth listen to my voice' (John 18:37). Just a short time before, at the Last Supper, the Lord had promised to his friends:

'When the Spirit of truth comes, he will lead you to the complete truth' (John 16:13). So, when we call on the Holy Spirit with Mary's help, we are led to listen to the voice of the Good Shepherd, the one who cares for his sheep and leads them to abundant pastures (cf. John 10:1-30). We may consider calling disciples 'sheep' a tad demeaning. After all, sheep are rather clueless, if adorable creatures, characterised by a herd mentality – doesn't the use of this image contradict our uniqueness and the counter-cultural nature of discipleship? Indeed, but there are at least three qualities sheep have that the Lord asks for in his disciples: they are called to trust, listen, and follow. When we learn to trust the Master, we find peace in troubled times; think of a flock happily grazing, serene in the knowledge of the Shepherd's protection. When we listen to his voice, he leads us out (*e-ducare* in Latin, the origin of the term 'educate') of our stressful situations and our messes to regain the path to the kingdom. When we follow him, believing that he is the Way, he will show us the right road home. As Pope Francis states in *Gaudete et Exsultate* 15:

> In the Church, holy yet made up of sinners, you will find everything you need to grow towards holiness. The Lord has bestowed on the Church the gifts of scripture, the

sacraments, holy places, living communities, the witness of the saints and a multifaceted beauty that proceeds from God's love, 'like a bride bedecked with jewels' (Isaiah 61:10).

To the witness of the saints we can add the life stories of many Christian men and women whose Spirit-filled lives have inspired us. For example, reading 'He Leadeth Me' by Walter J. Ciszek S.J. – who spent twenty-three years in Soviet prisons and labour camps – shows us how the Good Shepherd can bring strength in even the most desperate conditions, and reminds us never to take religious freedom for granted. 'May the God of hope bring you such joy and peace in your faith that the power of the Holy Spirit will remove all bounds to hope' (Romans 15:13).

Already God sees us in glory

It's not only the great heroes of the persecuted churches who inspire others. My late friend Pat (to whom this book is dedicated) battled cancer courageously for many months, with great faith and patience. He kept on his mobile phone a quote from St Thérèse: 'Time is but a shadow, a dream; already God sees us in glory and takes joy in our eternal beatitude. How this thought helps my soul! I understand then why he lets us suffer'. These words must have given him great joy and consolation. The Spirit leads us to the fullness of truth, not only by reminding us of all that Jesus has said in the Gospel (cf. John 16:13 and 14:26) but also by moving the saints to write of their experiences, and nudging us to share their words. How often someone has sent me a biblical quote or a thought from the saints, just when it was most needed. *Already God sees us in glory*: maybe you know someone who would benefit from reading this line today.

4. The Assumption of Mary: Drawn by Love (Apocalypse 12:1-6)

'A great sign appeared in heaven': we might quibble at the non-Scriptural insertion of the final two glorious mysteries of the Rosary, but God has his reasons. He could have made his existence to the world so evident that no one would doubt his presence, but then would we have been truly free to choose him in faith? In a comparable way, he seemed to want to give us glimpses of Mary's role in salvation history; yet in a discreet, almost hidden manner, trusting that the Church would elaborate on her mystery over time.

Learning to love: this has been our central theme and quest, and Mary is at its heart, since she enjoys a pivotal role in the love story between God and the human race. Through our efforts to recite the Rosary she is with us to help us to pray, for prayer is the true language of love. We know that when his disciples pleaded with Jesus, 'Lord, teach us to pray' (Luke 11:1), he taught them the *Our Father*; we could add that every word and action of Christ in the Gospel is an answer to this request. We've seen how he gave us his own mother at the Cross, through the beloved disciple: 'This is your mother' (John 19:27). So as we strive to welcome Mary into our homes and into our hearts, we can be certain she brings us on a journey of faith, which can also be used as an acronym: Fantastic Adventure In Trusting Him!

At the Ascension, Jesus was taken up by the glory of the Father into heaven; Mary's Assumption is a kind of first-fruits or anticipation of the ultimate pathway God desires for all his children. Leaving aside for now the mysterious destinies of Enoch and Elijah mentioned in the Old Testament, Mary alone among all creatures is already in heaven with a glorified body. It is true that the souls of the saints await their new bodies at the end of time. In a way, we can even now be there in the heavenly realms in spirit, for she wants to bring a taste of this celestial bliss to her poor, wandering children 'mourning and weeping in this vale of tears.' Mary imparts to us this yearning for God which is ingrained into our deepest being: 'Like the deer that yearns for running streams, so my soul is yearning for you, my God' (Psalms 41:2). Apparently, a deer seeks water for two reasons: to quench its thirst, and also to make predators lose its scent by crossing a stream. Only God can satisfy the thirst for authentic love within us, and at the same time protect us from all evil. Mary, enjoying the fullness of glory in heaven, enfolded in the radiant light of the Trinity, is still – and even more so – Mother of the Church, mother of each one of God's children. She helps those who turn to her to see clearly, to grasp which of our life choices lead us to God – thus satisfying our thirst – and which ones lead us away from him. We all have a sad tendency to seek more *stuff*, more *fun* and more *control* in the things of this world; she doesn't want us to hear the terrible condemnation of the Lord made through the prophet Jeremiah: 'they have abandoned me, the fountain of living water, only to dig cisterns for themselves, leaky cisterns that hold no water' (2:13). Mary echoes and magnifies above all the words of her Son: 'If you only knew what God is offering … you would have been the one to ask, and he would have given you living water' (John 4:10).

Le Bronzing

Various saints remind us how God is drawn in a special way to those who pray to Mary. Saint John Eudes explains, 'After the veneration we owe to the divine majesty of God, we cannot render a greater service to Jesus Christ or do anything more pleasing to him than to serve and honour his most worthy Mother'. Since her life on earth responded wholeheartedly to God's will, we can be sure that her protection and intercession on our behalf are most powerful. We'd love to have seen her at prayer, after Pentecost, when she lived as completely united to Jesus as when he was on the earth. Watching her pray, the apostles must have been elevated, inspired and emboldened to become missionaries; her presence at the very birth of the Church is still a reality for us today. Prayer can be compared to sunbathing – the French term *le bronzing* hints at the active side of the experience – since its effects are not immediately seen, but eventually produce, with the grace of God, a kind of tan for the soul. As St Basil the Great wrote in the fourth century: 'Like the sunshine, which permeates all the atmosphere, spreading over land and sea, and yet is enjoyed by each person as though it were for him alone, so the Spirit pours forth his grace in full measure, sufficient for all, and yet is present as though exclusively to everyone who can receive him'. Praying with Mary, the pure creature who is our light and guiding star, we can experience this divine sunshine and truly come to know that we are loved; the glory of the invisible God is upon us, and can indeed be *enjoyed by each person as though it were for him or her alone* – 'because you are precious in my eyes, because you are honoured and I love you' (Isaiah 43:4).

To eternity ... and beyond

The prophet Elijah is one of my favourite characters from the Old Testament. After encountering God in a cave, in the 'gentle breeze' (cf. 1 Kings 19:9-18), he is not afraid to tackle corrupt kings and false prophets, and after choosing Elisha as his successor, is apparently assumed into heaven. 'As they walked on, talking as they went, a chariot of fire appeared and horses of fire, coming between the two of them, and Elijah went up to heaven in the whirlwind' (2 Kings 2:11). The Carmelite order was born of the intuition of Elijah's spiritual closeness to Mary, and named after the mountain where Elijah sacrificed to God and proved the deception of the prophets of Baal (cf. 1 Kings 18-40). Every time we recite the Rosary, we are in a way led up the mountain with Mary, anticipating the raising up